The family, the victims, the murderer

- **Harry Hitchcock,** the Benson patriarch—gave his family millions but ignored their souls

- **Margaret Benson,** his daughter—the domineering mother who ruled with an iron fist in a velvet glove

- **Scott Benson,** her illegitimate grandson—died without knowing the sordid truth about his real identity

- **Carol Kendal,** the lone survivor—her beauty was ravaged by the blast, her testimony helped convict her own brother

- **Steven Benson,** heir to the family fortune—would do anything to succeed—including commit murder.

"THE SERPENT'S TOOTH SUCCESSFULLY IMMERSES THE READER IN THE TENSION AND TRAGEDY OF THE BENSON FAMILY MURDERS."
                                            —*Milwaukee Sentinel*

The Serpent's Tooth

Christopher P. Andersen

ST. MARTIN'S PRESS/NEW YORK

In loving memory of
Eunice Haines Peterson

THE SERPENT'S TOOTH

Copyright © 1987 by Christopher P. Andersen

Photo insert researched and edited by Vincent Virga

Published by arrangement with Harper & Row, Publishers, Inc.

Library of Congress Catalog Card Number: 86-46040

ISBN: 0-312-90541-6   Can. ISBN: 0-312-90542-4

Printed in the United States of America

First St. Martin's Press mass market edition/February 1988

10 9 8 7 6 5 4 3 2 1

Contents

Acknowledgments

For their enthusiasm and for their guidance, I am indebted to Lawrence Ashmead and Margaret Wimberger of Harper & Row and to my agent, Ellen Levine. My thanks also to Vincent Virga, Nancy Benson, Michael Minney, Janet Lee Hitchcock Murphy, Wayne Kerr, Kim Beegle, Joseph D'Allesandro, Ron Bolling, Ad Crable and Edward and Jeanette Andersen. I am especially grateful to Valerie and Kate, and to Linda Marx, without whose help *The Serpent's Tooth* could not have been written.

How sharper than a serpent's tooth it is
To have a thankless child!

—KING LEAR

Prologue

Naples, Florida
July 9, 1985

THERE WAS AN EERILY QUIET, almost serene airspace between Carol Lynn and the shimmering orange-red walls
of the tunnel. At least it seemed like a tunnel to her,
though it was happening all so quickly—in the turn of an
ignition key—that she could only guess at the properties
of this force that now encircled her. But she knew that it
was malevolent, and that it was pressing her back into the
seat, pulling her down into a place she did not want to
go. She wondered in that split second what it was she
might have touched, as she sat there in the back of the
Chevrolet Suburban wagon, to electrocute her, for this is
what she imagined it was like to be electrocuted. She
screamed. Mother and Scott are sitting there in the front
seat, she thought. Why don't they help me? Can't they
see I'm being electrocuted?

Carol Lynn opened her eyes—only now did she realize

that the shock of whatever it was had forced them shut—
and turned her head to the left, just enough to see Scott,
sprawled face-up perpendicular to the car, his left arm
raised above his head, his eyes not quite closed. His light-
blue swim trunks with the single one-dollar bill in the right
rear pocket no longer matched the short-sleeved plaid
shirt that his blood had now turned a vivid purple. His
face seemed unmarked, yet Carol Lynn knew her brother
was dead. What she could not see was that the blast had
ripped through Scott's back, exposing his intestines and
spleen; a white shard of shattered thighbone protruded
through the blood-soaked trunks. It was then that she realized the tunnel was in fact a fireball, and that she had
to get out of the car, to escape the tongues of flame that
now licked up and around the front seat. But she could
not see her hands. How am I going to get out if my hands
are burned off? she thought. How will I catch myself when
I hit the ground? No time. Leading with her left shoulder,
she held her breath and hurled herself to the ground.

Chuck Meyer was just getting ready to tee off on the
third hole of Naples' Quail Creek golf course when the
sound of the explosion thundered across the fairway at
precisely nine-eighteen that morning. More goddamned
construction noise, Meyer thought—until he saw the col-
umn of black smoke billow above the barrel-tiled roof of
the Benson house, not 140 feet away. Still clutching his
five iron in his right hand, the retired publishing executive
sprinted through the brush and around the side of the
house to the circular drive paved with coral-colored river
rock.

What had once been the family Suburban—it bore
scant resemblance to any kind of vehicle now—was a rag-
ing inferno as flames shot sixty feet up from the skeleton-

2

ized steel wreckage into the airless Florida sky. Meyer knew instantly that Scott was dead. On the other side of the Suburban, Carol Lynn's mother, Margaret Benson, lay crumpled in a bed of red hibiscus—not far from her forty-thousand-dollar bronze-toned Porsche 928. The left side of Margaret's head and all of her once-beautiful face had been ripped away. There was a gaping cavity where her breasts had been, but her limbs were intact. The sock had been blown off her left foot. On her left hand was the gold ring she always wore—the one with a single spindle-shaped aquamarine surrounded by six smaller diamonds, which her husband had given her. Lying there in the flower bed, Margaret might have been a rag doll torn apart and cast aside by a spoiled and angry child.

He could not help Scott or Margaret—no one could now—but Chuck Meyer heard Carol Lynn's screams and spun around to see her lying on the ground. She had somehow managed to sit up, pull her burning blouse off over her head and toss it away. For a time that seemed like an eternity to her, Carol Lynn was there facing the house, propped up by one arm like the subject of Andrew Wyeth's haunting *Christina's World*. Steven suddenly materialized on the front steps. For a moment he stood motionless. Then, in an instant, his eyes widened, his mouth dropped. He ran back into the house. "Steven, *help me*," Carol Lynn cried out. Where is Steven going? she wondered. Why isn't my brother helping me?

Inside the house, in the back bedroom she shared with Scott, Kim had been jolted awake. Turning to see crumpled bedsheets where Scott had been only minutes earlier, she jumped to her feet and looked out the window. She could not see the driveway from this vantage point, only a garbage truck parked on the street. Kim assumed the

noise that had awakened her must have come from the
truck—until she saw Meyer rushing toward the driveway.
Oh, God, she thought. Scott!

Meyer grabbed Carol Lynn under the arms and had
managed to pull her perhaps a dozen feet from the holo-
caust when the second blast knocked them both to the
ground, shooting shrapnel through Meyer's arm and chest
and tearing off the end of his nose. Kim threw on some
clothes, rushed outside and saw Meyer wandering about
in a daze, still clasping his golf club. Steven was sitting on
the front step of the house, holding his head in his hands
and moaning strangely. The beige van, parked just a yard
or two away, was splattered with blood and bits of flesh.
Kim bent over her lover's body and, sobbing hysterically,
ran over to Steven to tell him his brother was dead. Steven
said nothing.

Paul Hardy, whose father, a millionaire developer, had
built the exclusive Quail Creek subdivision, had just been
coming through the main security gate when it happened.
By the time he arrived, police were covering up the bodies.
One of the men from the garbage truck had led Carol Lynn
to safety across the street, and now she stood there alone
on the lawn. She refused to sit down, she said, because
there were bugs on the grass. The real reason, which Carol
Lynn could not bring herself to admit to anyone, was that
she feared she would die if she sat down. Her burns were
severe—so extensive, in fact, that within thirty minutes
she would be admitted to the hospital in critical condition,
but she thought to herself as she waited for the ambulance:
As long as I'm standing I'll be okay, I'll make it. Carol
Lynn remembered that the quick application of ice was the
best treatment for burns. When Kim raced out of the house

and handed her soaked towels instead, Carol Lynn flew
into a rage.

Hardy walked up to Carol Lynn, but before he could say anything she spoke. "My mother's dead, isn't she?" Hardy nodded. Carol Lynn then asked him to find her contact lens case. She did not want to pass out with her lenses in.

◆ ◆ ◆

Veterinary nurse Nancy Benson had just returned from her morning rounds to the dairy farms in and around Lancaster, Pennsylvania, when her brother called.

"Have you seen the news on TV?"

"No."

"Scott and Mrs. Benson were killed. Somebody blew up their car. Carol Lynn's in critical condition. Looks like Steve's okay."

Nancy felt as if the wind had been kicked out of her. She switched on the television and stood motionless in the center of her small living room, staring in disbelief at the parade of grotesque images that told the tragic story: aerial views of the Quail Creek house showing the blackened craters in the driveway where the bombs had detonated, the charred and twisted remains of the Chevy Suburban sitting in a police warehouse somewhere, the dated photos of the victims—Scott wearing a coat, tie and Prince Valiant haircut in his 1982 high school graduation picture, Margaret in a white knit tennis dress, racket under her right arm, squinting against the sun as she posed in front of her home just a few months earlier.

There was no love lost between Nancy and the Bensons; she was only now, six years after her divorce from Steven, beginning to recover from the emotional strain that went hand in hand with being a member of the family, even if only a member by marriage. But she could still feel a wave of sadness wash over her. Nancy was convinced that this tremendous tragedy had something to do with Scott and his drugs. What else could it have been? Who else could have done this?

◆ ◆ ◆

Three miles away, at his home in Lancaster's tony School Lane Hills district, eighty-eight-year-old tobacco tycoon Harry Hitchcock picked up the telephone, and his own personal nightmare began. Just seventy-two minutes earlier, he was told, a bomb blast had ended the lives of his eldest daughter and his grandson. Hitchcock hung up the telephone and slumped into an overstuffed chair. His head was roaring. Who would want to kill Margaret and Scotty? *Why?* It was indeed a nightmare, he thought, a dream from which he would certainly awaken—from which he *must* awaken.

PART ONE

THE
FAMILY

"If rough seas make good captains,
then I qualify as an admiral."
—HARRY HITCHCOCK

Chapter 1

He was always "Boppa" when only family was around. The minute anyone construed as being an outsider stepped into the room, they suddenly shifted to the more conventional Papa or Pa, as if by revealing their real nickname for the patriarch they might in some way give up a little precious piece of themselves. That the old man, having built an empire practically on charm alone, could spawn such a guarded lot might have seemed incongruous. But if his legacy would prove eventually to be twisted and flawed, the same could not be said of Harry Hitchcock.

Harry was a textbook Horatio Alger case—part Ragged Dick and part Professor Harold Hill from *The Music Man*, a glowing, dapper, upright, smooth-talking, suspender-thumping example of what savvy and salesmanship and that homegrown all-American drive to succeed can accomplish. Sized up today, he looked every inch the contented retired tycoon—a man who, having played the biggest game in town fairly and won, was now quietly reveling in his role as wise and benevolent paterfamilias. Had he been a character in a Frank Capra film (and he might well have been), Harry would have been played by Guy Kibbee or Frank Morgan or any one of a dozen sweet-cheeked, cuddly old character actors who, between periodic checks of their pocket watches, cheerfully dispensed the wisdom of the ages. From his wavy thatch of thick white hair, matching bushy eyebrows and leprechaun-pink face, down to the wide-lapeled suit, correct striped tie and brown wing tips, he was the perfect picture of the American grandfather. Norman Rockwell, had he ever encountered Harry, would have had to look no further for a model of kindness incarnate to shine forth from a *Saturday Evening Post* cover. Born and bred in Baltimore, Harry had pursued his dream in Pennsylvania and found it here; so his politics could be described as self-made Middle Atlantic Republican conservative—no ideologue, but no namby-pamby William Scranton moderate, either. Giveaway liberals were about as welcome to Harry as budworms in his tulip beds.

It came as no surprise, then, that he was also an intensely religious man, given to quoting Scripture and—almost by way of apology whenever talk turned, as it so often did, to the sheer enormity of his personal fortune—lavishing praise on the Lord for bestowing on him so many material riches. Such words might have seemed more than a little insincere coming from anyone else whose pockets were said to jangle to the tune of perhaps one hundred million dollars, but not when they came from Harry Hitchcock.

He had become, for reasons of his own and decades before Watergate conspirators and reformed rock star druggies made the term fashionable, a bona fide born-

again Christian. It happened in 1959, while he attended a
Christian prayer breakfast in Baltimore. That year—the
year he moved from Baltimore to Lancaster—Harry joined
the First United Methodist Church and started his own
prayer group right here among the God-fearing Protes-
tants of Lancaster. Every fourth Sunday since, though the
venue might change—one month on folding chairs under
the basketball hoops in a high school auditorium, the next
in air-conditioned splendor at the Holiday Inn—Harry was
always on hand to trade bits of Scripture and more often
than not take to the plywood lectern as the Lord's emcee.

Here and there were a few younger faces, usually be-
longing to the same sort of men who became church ush-
ers or Rotarians for whom membership had its distinct
business advantages. Those under fifty owned the car
dealerships and the fast-food franchises, practiced den-
tistry or had climbed several rungs up the executive ladder
at one or another of the big corporations headquartered
here. They wore perforated white shoes and their sports
coats and slacks came in a blinding array of pastels, from
cranberry red to lime green, in the summer; the rest of the
year, three-piece gray pinstripes outnumbered solid blue
suits two to one. All played golf, tennis, or both, and most
were already bloated about the belly. They were garrulous
beyond their years, middle-aged before their time—and
this was a condition they embraced joyfully. What these
prematurely aging Christian males longed to be, of course,
were fat-cat burghers like Harry and his contemporaries—
men of commerce who had nothing left to prove. Contented men who, if you were to stand them up against a
wall and frisk them, would each be toting snapshots of
the grandchildren, a bottle of blood-pressure pills, the
keys to the Lincoln and less than fifty dollars in cash.

11

As he gloried in his Christian faith, Harry took great pride in his ability to make more than just his bank account grow. Anyone taking a leisurely weekend drive to gawk at the millionaires' mansions in School Lane Hills might well slow to a crawl in front of the brick Georgian manor on Wilson Drive or the pink-walled Italianate villa on Marietta Avenue. But the one address few could pass up was the comparatively modest colonial at 1510 Center Road. Flowing around the left-hand side of the Hitchcock house and spilling out almost onto the curb was a river of color: more than six hundred cotton-candy-pink azaleas, rhododendrons in lavender and white, daffodils, geraniums and hyacinths, flowering cherry trees and over one hundred species of tulips—more than fifty thousand spring flowers alone. On the lawn, Harry, who fancied himself something of a poet, had posted a few hand-lettered lines of heartfelt if clumsy verse:

> Come visit with us in our garden.
> You are welcome to walk on our sod.
> When you commune with our flowers
> You are getting closer to God.

If that didn't do the trick, Harry might put down his morning paper, tuck his bifocals in the pocket of his madras shirt, and walk across the lawn to extend a personal invitation to passersby. Then, patiently, he would sometimes take them on a tour of the garden. Most of the trees, he would tell them, are old friends he brought here from his home in Baltimore. In fact, with the help of a professional landscaper, he patterned this garden on that city's Sherwood Gardens. The informal, country-garden effect was achieved by taking a dozen bulbs from each box every fall and alternating them randomly. No, now that he's in his eighties, he doesn't do all the work—a horticultural student from Penn State maintains the grounds, helped out by some kids from Lancaster Bible College. Harry might also apologize for the lateness of the rhododendrons this spring—though the tulips are lasting longer than usual—and in passing point out that his daughters used to bring their children over to play on the emerald lawn that connected each "island" of blooms.

After Charlotte, his wife, died in September of 1981, Harry put up a small plaque dedicating the garden as a memorial to her—and their sixty-two years together. She had always called Harry's work on his magnificent gardens "just puttering."

To look at him now, Harry Hitchcock seemed about as rock-solid a foundation as anyone could want for either a business or a family. Yet one had but to look at the whole of his life to see that Harry was in truth, like most who succeed spectacularly, a man of passion and paradox.

Chapter 2

There was no more quintessentially American place and time than Baltimore at the turn of the century. Born there in 1897, on the eve of the Spanish-American War, Harry grew up in a bustling George M. Cohan world of high button shoes and bandstands, Stanley steamers and straw boaters and barbershop quartets. It was a time of opportunities, and before he was in long pants Harry would learn from a master how and when to seize them.

Harry's father, Walter T. Hitchcock, had been totally sightless since birth, so it seemed something short of logical when the entrepreneur opened Baltimore's second movie house in 1904. The Imperial Nickelodeon, as it was grandly called, was actually a simple storefront operation with a seating capacity of sixty, all perched on wooden folding chairs lent by the local YMCA. For his nickel, the paying customer got to see Mary Pickford and William S. Hart flicker across a muslin screen, not to mention a few minutes of live entertainment—Hitchcock, billed as "Baltimore's Blind Singer-Professor," banging away at a rickety upright as he belted out popular ditties of the day like "My Wild Irish Rose" and "A Shanty in Old Shanty Town." Each tune was accompanied by an illustrated slide.

Harry, just seven, had his part to play. He stood behind the screen, improvising sound effects for each onereeler. Hitchcock senior also flashed a few advertisements on the screen before the show, like the one for Smith Brothers. They paid for the ad with cough drops. Little Harry would hawk them during intermission. Mom was cashier.

A devout believer in promotion, "Professor" Hitchcock hung a larger-than-life full-color poster of himself in the window. A five-foot-long horn hooked up to a brand-new Columbia cylinder phonograph blasted Sousa marches from atop the Imperial's transom—hardly something to escape the notice of passersby.

Still, after less than a year a bigger and better theater opened across the street—one of more than a hundred that sprung up around Baltimore overnight—forcing the Imperial Nickelodeon out of business and giving Harry his first taste of failure. It was only a taste; as soon as the competition started hiring vaudeville acts, the Professor became a booking agent—one of the region's most successful, it would turn out.

The blind professor was a churchgoer, a dreamer and above all a consummate salesman. The eldest of his three sons would inherit all these traits, and though he owed much to Methodist Sunday school (not long after his mother died Harry took the Lincoln-Lee pledge against smoking and drinking at age 12), for nearly a half century his spiritual well-being would take a back seat to his ambition. In the sixth grade, Harry dropped out of school and took a job at a mail-order house called the Baltimore Bargain House.

In America's pre-crash heyday, it seemed as if the whole country was puffing on a big fat stogie right along with J. P. Morgan. Harry was well into his twenties and married to Charlotte Brown (they met at Baltimore Bargain House and he liked to say she was "the best bargain they ever had") by the time he joined the H. W. Winston Company. Traveling up and down the East Coast selling tobacco leaf to small cigar companies, Harry tackled the job with such zeal that within a few months the big boss in New York summoned him to discuss his future over lunch.

For Harry, the meal was a trying ordeal. This was his first time in so formal a restaurant. The waiters intimidated him, as did the French menu. He solved that by merely listening to his host harrumph his tongue-twisting order, then nodding: "I think I'll have the same."

As coffee was poured, the H. W. Winston pooh bah reached into his breast pocket and pulled out two Brobdingnagian black cigars. He handed one to Harry. Then the executive chewed off the end of his cigar, and Harry did the same. Harry thought he might be able to go through with it, but when the man offered him a light, Harry had to confess. "I don't smoke," he blurted out. This was a potentially embarrassing little fact that he had up to now managed to conceal from his employers. It seemed safe to assume that his career in the tobacco business had abruptly come to an end, but the executive seemed more amused than anything. The job in the company treasurer's office was still open, if Harry was interested. He was.

16

Harry's nonsmoker status was not the only thing that made him an oddity in the tobacco business. Harry did not know one leaf from another, and never pretended to. That, he felt, was best left to the experts. What the experts told him was that the dark, air-cured tobacco grown in Lancaster, Pennsylvania, made the best cigars.

Traditionally, cigar manufacturers were forced to travel to the tobacco-producing regions of the country and buy either at auction or straight from the growers themselves. By setting up a tobacco leaf trading company, Hitchcock could offer every cigar manufacturer a surefire way to short-circuit the system without sacrificing quality. The trading company would act as a clearinghouse: Hitchcock & Co. would take care of buying the crops, then would process the tobacco and deliver it to the manufacturers at a tidy profit.

Hitchcock went to the source—Lancaster County in central Pennsylvania, since the Civil War the country's largest producer of cigar tobacco. In 1927, he purchased the entire crop from the previous year and launched the Lancaster Leaf Tobacco Company in a small brick warehouse on Liberty Street in the town of Lancaster. Within six years, Lancaster Leaf was far and away the biggest dark-leaf trader in the world, supplying the tobacco for nearly every cigar manufacturer in the United States.

Astoundingly, business flourished even with the Great Depression. The image of a hobo holding up the frayed remains of a blackened stogie with a toothpick said as much about a cigar smoker's passionate yen for a good smoke as it did about grinding poverty. The cigar market grew during the 1930s, and with it Lancaster Leaf. Gradually, Hitchcock expanded his empire to include five new subsidiaries: a processing plant in Wisconsin, Viroqua Leaf

Tobacco, Inc.; a Philippine subsidiary; a European sales headquarters in Belgium; a Connecticut packing plant; and Lanco Fill, Inc.

For the next three decades, Hitchcock would commute the eighty miles to Lancaster from Baltimore, where his wife, Charlotte, and their daughters, Margaret and Janet Lee, had their friends and their schools. It hardly mattered to Harry; he continued to live out of a suitcase, racking up fifty thousand miles a year on the road as he sweet-talked dozens of independent manufacturers sprinkled along the East Coast, as well as the majors, to buy from Lancaster Leaf. He was, like his father, the blind "singing professor," first and foremost a salesman.

Chapter 3

While the girls were growing up in suburban Baltimore, Charlotte Hitchcock took her husband's long absences in stride. As soft-spoken and shy as Harry was outgoing, Mrs. Hitchcock willingly embraced the traditional role of housewife and mother, serving as the emotional anchor for the family—a constant and caring presence in her daughters' lives. Charlotte made a point of never complaining about their father's interminable weeks and months on the road.

Margaret was only ten and little Janet Lee was still in the nursery when Harry pocketed his first million, and though the Hitchcocks lived comfortably—no mean feat at the height of the Depression—there was no ostentatious show of wealth. The children were as blissfully unaware of their family's lofty financial status as were the neighbors, and that meant they could enjoy a normal childhood.

The substantial age difference between the two girls precluded any intense sibling rivalry, but it also meant that as a child Janet Lee felt a certain distance from Margaret.

Margaret, after all, was already halfway through high school before Janet Lee had spent a single day in kindergarten; at times, Margaret seemed less like a sister and more like a third parent.

Janet Lee had other reasons to be at least a little bit in awe of her big sister: Margaret was beautiful. Slender, stylishly turned out and naturally poised, she bore a striking resemblance to the young Eleanor Parker. And she was smart, a straight-A student at Baltimore's Eastern High who went on to study biology at Maryland's Goucher College, graduating with a bachelor's degree in 1943.

It seemed only natural that Margaret would fall for Edward Benson. A onetime department store salesman who had risen to the rank of captain in the Army Air Corps during World War II, tall, dark-haired, chisel-jawed Benson cut a dashing figure in his officer's uniform when mutual friends introduced him to Margaret at a party. She was attracted by his air of confidence and his easy, unaffected charm—qualities he shared with her father. To him, she was an enticing blend of beauty, brains—women with college degrees in science were still something of a rarity in 1943—and money. They danced to Glenn Miller and Artie Shaw, drank champagne cocktails at the country club, and when they joined the ranks of thousands of young wartime marrieds it surprised absolutely no one.

Marrying the boss's daughter assured Benny of a permanent place in the executive hierarchy of Lancaster Leaf after his discharge from the service, and from a purely business standpoint Harry Hitchcock could not have wished for a better son-in-law. Behind the charm, Benson was every inch the perfectionist—a chain-smoking, Scotch-drinking, gray-flannel-suited cynosure of the postwar executive. As driven as his father-in-law, Benny began to shoulder the heavy burden of Lancaster Leaf's fledgling chewing tobacco business and the firm's embryonic foreign operations, globe-trotting to such far-flung locales as Nigeria, Indonesia, Puerto Rico, the Philippines, the Dominican Republic and Europe.

The parallels between Margaret's married life and that of her mother were fast becoming apparent. Margaret was in awe of her husband's business acumen, and she accepted without question his obsession with work, his late nights at the office, the countless trips out of town. She would, in all probability, have been disappointed in the man she married if he hadn't shown that he was willing to work at least as hard as Harry to make the family enterprise an even greater success.

Margaret also had a firm notion of where she fit into the picture and, like her mother before her, quickly began staking out her own domain at home. The newlyweds wasted no time starting a family. On July 8, 1944, at the beginning of what was to be one of Baltimore's worst heat waves, Mrs. Edward Benson gave birth to the couple's first child, a daughter. They named her Carol Lynn. Following her mother's example, Margaret made a conscious decision to put a comfortable distance between her offspring. The towheaded baby girl with the Kewpie doll cheeks proved as precocious as her forebears—walking, talking, learning to read earlier than most other children—in all probability because for the first seven years of her life she was essentially raised as an only child, the sole focus of the family's attentions and affections.

There was an added dividend for Margaret: With only one tyke occasionally tugging at her hem, Mrs. Edward Benson could see to it that she and her husband had a suitable social life—or at least whatever social life they could piece together when he wasn't consumed with work. They seemed a perfect couple to those who knew them then—he the undisputed head of the family and the very last word on all matters financial, she the final authority on practically everything else. They were strong, at times overbearing figures in their concentric worlds, but where those worlds overlapped there appeared to be little conflict. They understood each other.

◆ ◆ ◆

Edward Benson's single-minded determination to make Lancaster Leaf a global empire notwithstanding, the company was still in many ways very much a one-man show, and after a quarter century that burden was taking a fearsome toll on the founder. Harry decided to at least take a breather. On the first Saturday after Labor Day, 1950, he got together ten fishermen friends and chartered a party boat, the *Priscilla*, out of Ocean City, Maryland. It turned out to be such an unforgettable excursion that Harry would later write a first-person article about it for the Lancaster *New Era*. He was sitting in a deck chair at the stern, fifteen miles offshore, when, Harry wrote, "Suddenly the boat shook as if it were in a collision, and immediately blood gushed from my right leg. I instinctively said, 'I am shot.' I do not know why . . . no other boats were in view, and as far as we could see no planes in the air."

Harry was bleeding profusely, but his friends tied on a tourniquet and offered him the only painkiller on board—a bottle of Scotch. "I almost," Harry said in the *New Era*, "but not quite, had my first drink." An ambulance waiting on shore took him straight to the hospital, and the next day he was released with his leg in a cast.

Local papers had a field day with the "Mystery Bullet," and Harry was just as baffled as they were until six weeks later. He learned that his boat had inadvertently strayed into a restricted area where Maryland air national guardsmen were engaged in target practice. So much, it seemed, for R & R.

◆ ◆ ◆

Still, the pressure mounted, until in 1955, while working alone in his office, Harry collapsed from exhaustion. He ignored the warning, and collapsed again. Physically and emotionally drained, for the first time in his life Harry took a long hard look at what his ambition had cost him. He had missed his daughters' growing up, and precious years with Charlotte.

It was in 1959 that Harry accepted an invitation to a prayer breakfast in Baltimore. There, surrounded by other men who had come perilously close to losing their humanity in search of the almighty buck, Harry ran across the line of Scripture that altered the course of his life: "For what is a man profited, if he shall gain the whole world, and lose his own soul?" Harry was already worth tens of millions; it was time to set the wheels in motion to turn over Lancaster Leaf to his son-in-law Edward Benson.

Chapter 4

Steven stared out the car window at the young women skipping hand in hand along the roadside. They wore long kelly-green skirts that brushed the tops of their shoes, black aprons and starched white bonnets. Edward Benson had moved his family to Lancaster to be closer to company headquarters two years earlier, in 1953, but little Steve was still enthralled by the strangely dressed creatures. To a four-year-old boy who wore a coonskin cap and watched *Leave It to Beaver*, these Amish girls might as well have come from the far side of the moon.

They were members of the Dutch Protestant sect whose gentle ways and curious customs—decoration, machinery and violence of any sort all *verboten*—have since been chronicled in films like *Friendly Persuasion* and *Witness*. Against the backdrop of Lancaster County's shining silver silos and clapboard farmhouses, the bewhiskered Amish fathers in their horse-drawn buggies seem as oblivious to the motorcycles and pickups that speed past as they are to the condos, satellite dishes and fast-food outlets that have sprouted around them. Indeed, even knickknack shops topped by billboards rudely advertising "Amish Stuff" do not appear to offend them, so dependent is the local economy on the tourist trade.

By 1959, when Harry and Charlotte decided it was finally time to stop commuting from Maryland and join Margaret and Benny (Janet Lee and her husband had already made the move, in 1957) nearer the source of the family fortune, the Amish were already a national attraction. But there was far more to the charm of Lancaster, a city of eighteenth-century brick houses with delft-blue shutters, Civil War monuments and narrow streets named after royal titles (King, Queen, East Duke) and fruit (West Orange, Cherry, Strawberry, Lime, Plum). The pillared antebellum mansions and Georgian estates sprinkled like gold dust through School Lane Hills rivaled the finest homes of the nearby Main Line, outside Philadelphia. Topping the list of fashionable School Lane Hills addresses was Wheatland, the sprawling Georgian estate of James Buchanan, fifteenth United States President and, as Lancaster folk are fond of pointing out, the only bachelor ever to occupy the White House.

With Benny away on business much of the time, Margaret threw herself into designing their School Lane Hills dream house at 1515 Ridge Road—a seventeen-room mansion with a mahogany-paneled study for Benny, ivory statuary, tennis courts, greenhouse and, for an added touch of opulence, five fourteen-carat-gold doorknobs. When Margaret decided the free-form swimming pool was too small, she had an Olympic-sized pool and cabana built on another part of the property. Then she transformed the old pool into a Japanese pond, complete with an arched wooden footbridge, bonzai trees, carp and a waterfall.

Projects like these helped fill in the empty days when Benny was away, and with Harry and Charlotte now living in the white clapboard house directly behind theirs, Margaret was thrilled. Maybe this was a chance for them to make up for some of that lost time, those years when Harry missed school pageants and birthdays because he was off somewhere talking a mom-and-pop operation into buying his tobacco.

Sadly, Margaret could not keep history from repeating itself with her own children. Because Harry was saddling Benny with more and more responsibility, her husband became increasingly distant emotionally as well as physically. It did not seem to bother Carol Lynn, perhaps because on those rare occasions when he was around, Benny doted on his beautiful, brainy daughter. She had, in fact, emerged from a chubby postadolescence to resemble the young Grace Kelly, and an outgoing disposition inherited from Harry made her one of the most popular kids in school.

Steven was another matter. Father (it was always "Father" and "Mother"—never "Mom" or "Dad") was too busy with work to take the time to play catch, fish, teach him how to ride a bike or do any of the things other fathers did with their sons. Even when he was home, Steven's father made little effort to get close to his son, and that indifference cut deep into the boy's psyche. It was a wound that would never heal.

Margaret did the only thing she knew how to do to make it up to the children. She indulged them. Every Christmas, for instance, became an orgy of gift giving as Santa lavished present after present on Carol Lynn and

Steven. Packages were opened according to age, youngest first, and the ritual would last an entire day. Janet Lee, now married herself but still very much Margaret's adoring little sister, would sit next to the tinsel-laden tree and watch in amazement as Carol Lynn tried on expensive dresses and Steven played with elaborate electronic toys and games that sometimes cost hundreds of dollars. Nevertheless, it was not much of a bargain in lieu of a father.

There seemed little doubt that Steven, already as introverted as his sister was outgoing, grew increasingly resentful of the attention lavished upon Carol Lynn at his expense. He bottled up his true feelings, but even to the casual observer it must have been clear that their relationship—if not outwardly any more hostile than most between big sister and little brother—could not be described as a particularly warm and loving one.

While Carol Lynn started driving to high school in her own red convertible, Steven dutifully attended Junior Cotillion, where every week he learned to waltz and foxtrot and wear white gloves. But when he wasn't training to be a little gentleman, Steven also pursued his passion for tinkering. No one knew where he got the knack—Harry and Benny both barely knew how to use a screwdriver—but the boy was such a technical whiz that at Lancaster Country Day School he was already building radios and other devices from kits. One day when he was ten, Margaret peeked into her son's room to see what he was working on. He had, to her astonishment, built his own television set. Later, Benny would come home to find that Steven had rigged an elevator to take him up to his tree house.

The talent would come in handy around all the Benson

27

households. As a teenager and into adulthood, Steven
would constantly be installing and upgrading security sys-
tems, intercoms, stereos, cable and telephone wiring, not
only at the house at 1515 Ridge Road, but also at the beach
house in Ventnor near Atlantic City, and the ski lodge in
the Laurentians outside Montreal. He even wired up the
forty-four-foot family yacht *Marlynn* (for Margaret and
Carol Lynn), which plied the waters of Chesapeake Bay.
Edward Benson would finance his son's interest in gadgets
for now, but he viewed such tinkering with remote disdain. If he gave any thought to Steven at all, it was to fret
about the boy's apparent lack of interest in business—
namely, *the* business. Why else did they think he was
pouring his blood into Lancaster Leaf, Benny wondered,
if not someday to be able to turn it over to his son?

Benny somehow managed to find the time, however,
to drive to Atlantic City's Pleasantville Yacht Club and
watch Carol Lynn win her first beauty pageant. She went
on to be crowned Miss Atlantic City, and when she made
it to the finals at the Miss New Jersey contest, Benny sat
transfixed as Carol Lynn, dressed in a blue velvet gown,
stood on the stage and delivered a two-and-a-half minute
soliloquy from *Romeo and Juliet*. The judges were impressed by the little rich girl's unaffected "sweetness"; she
made second runner-up. Not a bad showing by any
means, but Carol Lynn was accustomed to winning and
took her defeat seriously. Her days as a beauty queen
over, the sweet girl in the blue velvet gown packed for
college in Texas. She would return with more than just a
degree.

Chapter 5

Like other wives of rich and powerful men in 1963, Margaret knew instinctively that her role in life was to jealously guard that elusive yet all-important possession known as one's "place in the community." She held bridge parties for the Women's Symphony Association and teas for the hospital auxiliary in her meticulously decorated pink and gray pseudo-Victorian living room. She modeled chic wool suits and sequined evening gowns at the Lancaster County Horse Show and threw cocktail parties for her dance group, the Quadrille Club. She was a fixture in the society pages of the Lancaster *New Era* and the *Intelligencer-Journal*. She was chairman of the American Red Cross Auxiliary. Yet she was never completely embraced by the city's *grandes dames*, some of whom could trace their roots in Lancaster to before the American Revolution. Margaret chafed, for example, at never being asked to join the Junior League. And while their daughters were thrown lavish coming-out parties, Lancaster bluebloods never asked Carol Lynn to become a debutante. Still, Margaret made the best of her situation, periodically taking pleasure in turning down requests for charitable contributions from those committeewomen who had snubbed her.

The Old Guard's attitude notwithstanding, Margaret occupied a sufficiently lofty place in the town's social hierarchy. The baby threatened all that. Margaret knew all too well that the social powers-that-be in Lancaster would hardly be expected to handle the birth of Carol Lynn's illegitimate child with grace and understanding. These were still the days when teenagers went so far as to commit suicide rather than face the unbearable shame of an out-of-wedlock pregnancy. How could this be happening? Margaret asked herself again and again. What had she done to deserve it? Tears of frustration soon gave way to panic. If word got out, the stigma would certainly spell an abrupt and unseemly end to Margaret's brilliant social career. Yet there was no reason anyone in Lancaster had to know about Carol Lynn's baby. The fact that Carol Lynn attended college in Texas made it relatively easy for the family to conceal her situation, and after she gave birth to her love child on Christmas Day, 1963, in Baltimore, Margaret spirited him away to his new home in Lancaster.

❖ ❖ ❖

Steven was just thirteen, an eighth grader at Lancaster Township Junior High, and old enough, Margaret felt, to handle the truth. She sat her son down and explained to him that the infant squalling in the upstairs guest room was Carol Lynn's little boy, but that absolutely no one under any circumstances was to know. From now on he was to tell anyone who asked that he had a new, adopted baby brother, and the baby's name was Scott—Scott Roland Benson. Steven nodded, as if it were actually possible for a thirteen-year-old boy to fully comprehend such things—that he was in reality Scott's uncle—but Margaret seemed satisfied. She knew it would be hard on Steven at first, but she also knew she could count on him. He was, she always told the other society wives, an obedient little boy. As for caring for an infant, there were always servants around to handle the diaper changes and feeding and that sort of thing. Now, whenever her friends commented on the considerable age differences between her children, Margaret would explain that she "spaced them out because children can be such a bother." That first night, the cries of Steven's newly arrived baby "brother" filled the house. For Steven, sleep would never again come quite as easily as it once had.

Chapter 6

Mike Minney and Tom Schelling made a point of not noticing when Steve Benson made his grand arrival every school morning, roaring past his book-toting classmates in a flame-red Mercedes 280SL to the student parking lot behind McCaskey High. Like many of the built-to-last public schools dating from the 1930s, McCaskey had an institutional facade centered around a brick tower. It also had a purple-walled, gilt-domed, mosaic-tiled art deco interior, parts of which resembled the lounge of Radio City Musical Hall. The building was set back on a large plain, right across from the Triangle Car Wash and an Amoco station.

Most of the other working-class kids at McCaskey shared Mike Minney's early sentiments about Steven—that he was a snotty rich kid who drove flashy cars (he sometimes drove an MG) and threw money around to lord it over the rest of them as the grandson of the richest man in town. But Steven was looking for friends the only way he knew how—the same way his mother had sought and held his love, or at least his loyalty. He was looking to buy them. Lending somebody the 280SL to take a girl out on a date or inviting schoolmates to play tennis at the country club seemed a small price to pay for friendship.

Lynn Beyer was bouncy and chatty and had grown up with Steven. He liked her enough to give her his silver ID bracelet, and she was the envy of her girlfriends for having snagged the scion of Lancaster's richest family. Steven was her first beau, and she chose to excuse his pretensions as a sign of understandable insecurity over Scott.

Steven's girlfriend was not the only local who knew the real story behind Scotty's adoption. Far from it. Margaret had managed to keep the truth about Scotty from her own sister, Janet, until the boy was seven, but the Bensons' little secret was anything but a secret to most folks in Lancaster. It had not escaped them that Scotty and Carol Lynn shared the same Kewpie doll features ("God, they looked *exactly* alike," observed one family friend) or that it was most curious for Margaret to suddenly and inexplicably decide to adopt a boy when she was forty-one and already had two children—two heirs. Spontaneity was not something Margaret was famous for. It just, as a friend repeatedly put it, "didn't add up."

There was no way of knowing how deep Steven's resentment toward the interloper ran. It appeared to all who knew them to be one-sided: Scotty, who had been told he was adopted but nothing about the identity of his real mother, loved Steven, emulated him, wanted to grow up to be just like him.

But Steven had always been jealous of the affection Mother and Father lavished on Carol Lynn, and now he had to share what scraps of love were left with Carol Lynn's natural son. And they made Steven call the boy his "brother." Time did not heal his resentment. On the contrary, as he grew older, the situation grew more and more traumatic.

He had kept the hurt bottled up inside for the most part, though occasionally he complained to close friends that Scott had supplanted him as the favorite son. It infuriated Steven, for example, that Mother and Father had spent $20,000 on a new stereo for Scott, while Steven had been left to piece together his own. Lynn Beyer was one of the few allowed close enough to feel Steven's bitterness. Had he attended high school a few years later, Steven might have turned to drugs, as Scott eventually would. But this was before Vietnam or the Haight-Ashbury had their repercussions—a time when the only thing scandalous about the Beatles was the length of their hair. Pot was as rare at McCaskey as it was at practically every other high school in America.

Steven vented some of his pent-up anger by driving fast down the narrow roads that crisscrossed the farmlands around Lancaster. His squealing tires resulted in one citation for reckless driving (the charge was eventually dropped). He also took up judo, and liked to try out various flips and holds on some of the younger kids in the neighborhood—Lynn's brother Bob, for example—using sufficient force to induce them to keep their distance. But Steven's main release was to "fool around" with fireworks, or worse. A favorite testing ground was the large lot, not far from Steven's house, owned by a particularly cantankerous older couple who, in their ardent disdain for youth, seemed to take great pleasure in running kids off their property at the slightest provocation. Steven avenged himself by standing at the top of the hill behind their house and setting off his homemade pyrotechnics. Steven

also liked to experiment by a stream not far from Ridge
Road. Bob Beyer, who later became a lawyer, remembers
feeling the ground tremble as white smoke rose from the
parched creekbed.

"Now be good kids," Mrs. Beyer said to her daughter
as she walked out the door with Steven one Halloween
night, "and don't get arrested." Lynn wore a floppy
sweatshirt over jeans, and Steven handed her all the ord-
nance to carry in her ample pockets—dry cells, wires, tubing, alligator clips and dozens of firecrackers of varying
size. They drove out into the countryside, parked and
waited for the right target. Then Steven tossed the device
he'd assembled—onto the hood of a police car. They were
given a stern talking to but never actually arrested, Lynn
Beyer would later point out: "The whole thing was just
sort of swept under the suburban carpet—pushed under
the trees in the township."

Years later, Bob would come across some parapher-
nalia—dry cells, wires, the alligator clips—stuffed in the
back of one of the Beyers' closets. "Oh, this is Steven's
stuff," he said to himself. "I guess," he'd admit years later
to federal investigators, as if it had never really occurred
to him before, "you'd call them bombs."

Chapter 7

The bell rang and they streamed in, filling the gray tile-walled room with the din of war whoops and clanging metal lockers. The other guys pushed past Steven, who was in no rush to suit up. He couldn't, he told his physical education teacher—Steven had forgotten to bring his gym clothes. No matter; the teacher, one of those slightly-gone-to-seed local ex-jocks, told him with a grin that Steven could still play—in his underwear. The rest of the class broke into hoots of derision when Steven slunk out of the locker room in his Jockey shorts, in full view of the girls' class across the field. From that distance, the tears streaming down Steven's face could not be seen.

That year, Steven Benson was the only student to pose wearing a suit and tie for his sophomore class picture in the McCaskey yearbook, the *Echo*. The school's motto runs in bold type over his photo:

A FIRM FOUNDATION FOR THE BRIDGE TO SUCCESS

Nancy Ferguson and Steven hardly moved in the same
social circles. Nancy was a working-class girl from gritty
Cabbage Hill, the daughter of a printer who worked just
a few blocks from Lancaster Leaf headquarters. She had
seen Steven around, of course, behind the wheel of his
red Mercedes, and holding hands with Lynn Beyer. In
1968, however, they sat next to each other in their junior
social studies and English classes, and Steven asked her
out. He was different from the boys she was accustomed
to, flashy and egotistical, and her first inclination was to
turn him down flat. But Benson's body language—the
stiff, unsure way he held himself—told her there was a
sensitive, frightened boy beneath the facade. He had a
need to impress the other kids with his car, his house, but
it was more than that. The underlying message was a cry
for love, for friends, and to get them he used what he had:
money. He felt he couldn't just be himself and have someone love him, because he didn't like himself very much.
A part of Nancy felt sorry for Steven, sorry enough to say
yes to a first date, and to others after that. One of Nancy's
secret admirers, a chubby kid who sat near her in French
3, watched enviously as she hopped in Steven's sports car
and sped off. The chubby kid's name was Wayne Kerr.

Nancy had assumed that Steven's parents had starved
their son emotionally, and that this privation was at the
root of his gnawing self-doubt. So she was surprised at
the reception she received when Steven brought her home
to 1515 Ridge Road to meet Mother. Margaret seemed gen-
uinely warm toward Nancy, going out of her way to make
Steven's girl feel welcome and at ease around what must
have seemed to her luxury that rivaled Versailles. A

maid—one of the young girls Benny had sent over from Belgium each year—served them iced tea by the pool, and they chatted amiably about school and plans for the future.

There was no resemblance whatsoever between this lovely, caring woman and the soulless matriarch Nancy had conjured up in her imagination. She was beginning to wonder if she had been wrong all along about who was to blame for Steven's behavior. Perhaps Margaret's new-found tolerance had come in the wake of Carol Lynn's spur-of-the-moment marriage to a handsome Cypress Gardens waterskiing instructor named Tom Kendall. By comparison, Steven's romance with a hometown girl seemed rather tame.

◆ ◆ ◆

By the time he graduated from McCaskey in 1969, Steven had done well enough academically—particularly in subjects that came naturally to him, like chemistry and physics. He had also, despite his loner status, chalked up a surprising list of extracurricular credits: he had competed in junior varsity tennis, worked on the stage crew, even served on the student council and as home room president.

Both Nancy and Steven enrolled in Lancaster's Franklin and Marshall College—she as a special-education major and he to study business administration. Over the next two years, Steven dropped out of F&M and reenrolled twice without ever even officially declaring a major. He would wind up quitting a third and final time in August of 1972.

What he really wanted was to finally get his father's attention, and to do that he set up a landscaping business of his own, hiring his classmates to go out and cut the lawns of his millionaire neighbors in School Lane Hills. "Money meant success to that family," one would later point out. "Steve wanted to prove himself by running his own business." That did not prevent him, however, from letting Father bankroll the enterprise. Benny and Margaret seemed eager to see Steven make it as an entrepreneur.

Steven picked only the best equipment for his landscape business—the costliest riding mowers, power mowers, a truck. If there was such a thing as a left-handed automatic hedge clipper, he made sure they owned two—regardless of need. Steven was hell-bent on making the business work, and he soon had an added incentive: Father was now tightening the financial reins, demanding that Steven keep his expenses in check.

It surprised her as much as anyone, but Nancy now felt quite comfortable during her visits to the Benson estate. She looked forward to her talks with Mrs. Benson and with Peggy, the pretty young Belgian maid. One afternoon when Peggy answered the door, Nancy was shocked at how drawn and haggard she looked. "Are you feeling all right, Peggy?" she asked, but before the maid could answer, Margaret materialized at the head of the stairs. She asked Nancy to come up to the bedroom, and there Margaret shut the door behind them. Turning, Nancy looked into the contorted face of a stranger. This was not a side of Margaret she had ever seen before, or wanted ever to see again.

"How *dare* you imply that Peggy is overworked," Margaret screamed, her eyes wide with rage. "You are never, *never* to talk to my servants again like that, is that clear?"

"Well, Peggy looked a little tired," Nancy sputtered, "and I was just—"

"This is my house, Nancy, and you will not go around

talking to my maid as if I were working her into the ground. I hope you understand. Do you, Nancy? Do you understand?"

Nancy nodded feebly. This was her first real taste of life in the Benson household, and though in the back of her mind she knew that harsh reality would someday intervene, she had been eager to believe that the Bensons were a warm and caring family.

When Steven proposed to Nancy, it really never occurred to her to say anything but yes. As the wedding date approached, though, her anxieties mounted—not just the standard bridal butterflies in the stomach, but a gnawing fear that she was being drawn into a web of internecine intrigue. She had seen the hold Margaret and Benny had over Steven, that all either had to do was snap fingers and the dutiful eldest son would come running—running because his parents held the purse strings.

"The Bensons controlled the lives of their kids," Mike Minney, who was to become Steven's closest friend after his marriage to Nancy, would later explain. "It was carrot and stick from day one, and it permeated Steve's entire relationship with his parents. Everything was always in Daddy's name. The threat was always there that if Steven didn't behave the way his parents wanted, he would be cut off. I'm not sure anyone can survive positively in that atmosphere."

Neither was Nancy, but she convinced herself that she would be able to rescue Steven from his mother and father, and from his lack of self-esteem. She went through with the marriage in May of 1972, and Margaret and Edward bought them the kind of wedding present they deemed fitting for a girl of Nancy's social standing: a $29,000 green stucco row house in a blue-collar neighborhood a block from Franklin and Marshall College. F & M's huge turnip-shaped water towers loomed overhead.

Steven accepted the gift without complaint, and promptly added a few touches of his own. One day a neighbor, Esther Witmer, looked out her kitchen window and saw Steven climbing up a telephone pole at the rear of their narrow lot and hooking up a wire that would enable him to receive cable television signals—without paying, of course. Nancy worried whenever she saw a cable service truck drive by, certain they'd be caught.

Chapter 8

It was not long before Nancy felt the sting of her mother-in-law's manicured hand. Little Scotty looked up to his big brother and loved to spend whatever time he could with him at the green stucco house, but, Margaret pointed out, these visits were posing a threat to the boy's health. Nancy was a lifelong animal lover—in fact, for a long time she aspired to be a veterinarian—and she owned three cats. Scotty was allergic to cats. Therefore, Nancy would have to get rid of them. Nancy did not recall ever seeing Scotty show any severe allergic reaction when he visited; perhaps, she calmly suggested, something else was causing the problem, if indeed there was one.

Margaret disappeared for two days and returned to wave a signed doctor's report in Nancy's face. She had taken Scotty down to Johns Hopkins to be tested, and sure enough, he was allergic to cat dander. Margaret neglected to mention that he was also allergic, in varying degrees, to practically everything else. Margaret reminded Nancy that her in-laws still held the mortgage on the house, and issued an ultimatum: Get rid of the damned cats or get thrown out. Nancy had no choice.

That Mother would go to any lengths to be obeyed was just one more fact of life among the Bensons revealed to its newest member-by-marriage. For Nancy, the mysteries that once shrouded Lancaster's wealthiest family from public view were peeling away like the layers of an onion. Holiday dinners and other family get-togethers at 1515 Ridge Road might have been scripted by Edward Albee, as Carol Lynn and Margaret quarreled about everything from the table manners of Carol Lynn's own two small sons to the price of clothes. While guests like Nancy's parents cringed with embarrassment, Edward Benson was oblivious of the turmoil. He had what Nancy called "quiet power." On those rare occasions when he chose to speak, it was about things of importance to him—namely, business—and no one, not even Margaret, dared utter a syllable to contradict him. For his part, Steven tried his best to be invisible.

If she could hang by her fingertips to her own identity, Nancy felt there was reason to believe she could gradually help Steven find his. Earning her degree in special education from Millersville College in 1973, Nancy decided to enter the graduate program, working toward her Ph.D. by teaching brain-injured children.

For a time, Steven and Nancy managed to lead a life not unlike that of other young marrieds. They were perhaps closest to Nancy's cousin, who had wed their old McCaskey classmate Mike Minney, now a law student and aspiring Democratic party politico in overwhelmingly Republican Lancaster. Steven, an expert driver, had developed an interest in Formula One auto racing, and he and

43

Minney began making the trek each weekend to Watkins Glen, New York. Weekends Steve could be counted on to fix the grill for barbecues on the Minneys' back porch, and the evening was usually topped off with poker or *Saturday Night Live*. If the choice was cards, Minney had to set a pot limit and stick to it; Steven had a tendency to want to up the ante, pulling wads of cash from his pocket until everyone else was so intimidated they folded.

Mike, much to his astonishment, had actually grown fond of the rich kid he had scorned in high school. There was still the pretense: Steve made a point of chain-smoking Benson & Hedges cigarettes, and did nothing to discourage the widespread misconception that he was a Benson & Hedges heir—a curious piece of deception, since Lancaster Leaf was a far larger and more profitable enterprise. Steven had opened up as much with these friends as he had with anyone, yet this was only the narrowest breach in a wall of insecurity.

During one of their traditional backyard barbecues, the two couples were having so much fun that Mike decided to play a harmless prank on his buddy. Instead of dessert topping, Mike sprayed shaving cream on top of Steven's Jell-O. He served it, and waited for a reaction. It never came. Showing no sign that anything was wrong, Steven ate several bites, then without comment pushed the remainder aside. He was not ready to be made fun of; the teenager forced to play gym in his underwear was still alive within.

Whatever semblance of domestic serenity the young Bensons had together was short-lived. Under pressure from his parents, Steven was demanding that Nancy quit her job and settle into the roll of full-time housewife. Benson women didn't work, he told her—it was unseemly for her to have a job. What would his parents think? More to the point, what would they do if they decided he wasn't living up to their image of a son?

Nancy was not about to roll over. She did not need the Bensons' money, did not want it if it meant giving up her job. The landscaping business had not yet turned a profit, and it seemed to her that Steven was happy to have her extra income coming in to help him indulge his exorbitant taste in televisions, stereos and car phones. It seemed doubtful, in spite of his grandiose schemes, that her husband would ever be able to support them on his own unless he started to learn how to handle money. Ironically, this scion of one of the tobacco industry's great fortunes had never mastered budgeting and the paying of bills. Consequently, there were threats to cut off the phone and electricity because he had forgotten to mail in the checks. When he failed to meet his payroll or pay for machinery, Steven always told Nancy the same thing: "You sit here. I'm going to talk to Father." No matter what he did, there was always someone there to bail Steven out.

The tension mounted. Nancy believed in confrontation, in talking out problems. But Steven owed his very survival in his high-strung family to the avoidance of all direct conflict. There would be no discussion, no airing of feelings, no attempt at compromise. Frustrated, Nancy packed up and left Steven after only a few months of marriage.

She still wanted it to work, though, and when Steven's father asked to speak to her, she felt she owed it to him to listen. Of all the family members with the possible exception of Harry—who kept a benign distance from his own children's domestic problems even though he lived just over the back fence—Benny had been the kindest to

her. He took her hand and led her to the living room,
where Margaret sat waiting on a brocade-upholstered
Queen Anne chair. Sitting his daughter-in-law down,
Benny patiently explained that the marriage could survive
if she would just make one small sacrifice, if she would
quit her job and drop the whole notion of doing graduate
work. Steven was under a tremendous strain trying to get
the landscape company off the ground, and what he
needed now more than anything was the love and support
of a full-time wife. This was how he had been brought up,
how they had all been brought up. Was a job really more
important than her marriage? Throughout the entire
speech, Margaret sat listening intently, with her legs
primly crossed, her hands folded in her lap. She said
nothing.

Nancy relented, and in the process became Margaret's
newest project. Now that she was no longer wasting her
time working, Nancy could be transformed into a bona
fide Benson Woman. First stop: Margaret's hairdresser,
where Nancy's auburn hair was bleached ash-blond—the
precise shade of Margaret's hair, and of Carol Lynn's.
Then Margaret took her daughter-in-law to the country
club, bought her expensive golf outfits and her own top-
of-the-line golf clubs. She taught Nancy how to play
bridge, and mulled over the socially correct charity groups
the young Mrs. Steven Benson should join.

The sense of self that Nancy had clung to so desperately had slipped away. She no longer knew who she was.

Chapter 9

Once the landscaping company went belly-up in 1975, Steven knew he had no choice but to join Lancaster Leaf. His father was delighted; now free of distractions, his son could at last start to stake out a place for himself in the family firm, his birthright.

Lancaster Leaf's fortresslike home office is tucked away like a small-town secret on West Liberty Street, in the shadow of Armstrong Industries' sprawling world headquarters. You might never know it was here if you didn't spot the hand-carved wooden sign and the door flanked by two bronze carriage lanterns. These offices are actually the heart of a Dickensian warehouse complex, a confusion of brick, grime-smudged skylights and shattered panes that might just as well serve as the set for a regional-theater production of *Sweeney Todd* as headquarters for the world's largest tobacco distributor. A few steps from the genteel entrance to Lancaster Leaf's front office is an aptly named sawdust-on-the-floor joint, the Warehouse Tavern. Located one floor above the tavern is UAW Local 285.

As part of his apprenticeship at Lancaster Leaf, Steven was assigned first to the purchasing department, then to the technical side. It was here, as might have been predicted, that Steven got most involved, advising the company on how best to streamline its computer system and how to get rid of tobacco beetles in Lancaster Leaf's warehouses by installing an elaborate fogging system.

It was not enough. Steven felt the resentment of co-workers, and he began to wither in the long shadows of both his father and Harry Hitchcock. As Claude Martin, Edward Benson's successor as Lancaster Leaf president, would later recall, "Steven wanted to do something that he could say he had done on his own."

As if to reward their son and his wife for toeing the line, Margaret and Edward offered to spring for a bigger house. Of course, Margaret insisted on accompanying them on their house-hunting expeditions, and when Nancy balked at a contemporary her mother-in-law loved, Margaret exploded. "You don't like this house? This beautiful, *expensive* house? Maybe you've forgotten who's paying for it, Nancy dear."

Ultimately, they purchased a house even more to Mother's liking. It went for $77,655, had a stone-walled first floor, dormers and a prime address—1510 Ridge Road; it was directly across the street from the senior Bensons (Benny and Margaret would later buy a house around the corner for Carol Lynn and her two sons). Now when Mother called, Steven would only have to walk the fifty feet from his front door to hers. Margaret wasted no time telling Nancy what old pieces of theirs would be retrieved from the attic and the family warehouse to furnish her new home, and where to put them.

Another frequent guest was Scott, who at fourteen was already turning up in the afternoons glassy-eyed and in-

coherent. Steven cautioned him to stay away from drugs—
if for no other reason than that he might be caught. Given
the pressures in the Benson household, Scott's bizarre behavior was perhaps to be expected, but Nancy was becoming more and more concerned about Steven: He had
bought a serious-looking rifle (she assumed it was a machine gun) with a camouflage strap and slipped it under
their bed.

Nancy knew that if they could only get away on their
own and make a life for themselves on *their* terms, Steven
would begin to see he was a worthwhile person in his
own right—not just an appendage of Mother and Father.
Each night, Nancy begged Steven to break free from his
parents, and each night his response was the same: to get
up from the dinner table and read a magazine, then to
switch on the television set. When Nancy persisted in telling him their future together was on the line, he simply
turned up the volume on the TV, higher and higher until
the sound completely drowned out her pleas. Once, if
only for an instant, Nancy miraculously managed to break
through that invisible wall the real, frightened Steven still
crouched behind. She asked him if he was happy.

"I've never known what happiness is," he said.

"Then, Steven, what would make you happy? *Really*
happy?"

He paused before answering. "To make a million dollars," he said, "before I'm thirty."

It was not the answer Nancy wanted to hear.

◆ ◆ ◆

It had never before occurred to Nancy, not even when
things between them were at their worst, that Steven
might start seeing someone else. Although he never

49

shared his feelings with anyone, she knew he was in pain—so much so that he was being treated with drugs for a mild nervous breakdown. Still, he was able to do a lot of traveling to the Lancaster Leaf processing plant in Wisconsin, and when he was in town Steven commuted to the company's Mount Joy operation, a century-old one-time malt house situated in the hills about a half hour west of Lancaster.

Steven was also venturing out at night. One evening, she followed him—right to the apartment of a young brunette who, it turned out, worked as a secretary at the Mount Joy warehouse. Nancy was numb. She went straight to his parents and told them Steven was seeing another woman.

"We know," said Margaret. Nancy wanted desperately to erase the self-satisfied look from her mother-in-law's face.

"We had him followed some time ago," explained Edward Benson, controlling his cough just long enough to light up another cigarette. "We know who she is."

Nancy had already lost her identity. Now she felt she was losing her mind.

"Oh, don't worry, Nancy," Benny tried to reassure her. "These things happen. It's just a fling. He'll get over it."

The unspoken message was coming through loud and clear: You have only yourself to blame, Nancy. Maybe if you'd been a halfway decent wife, Steven wouldn't be straying.

Nancy tried to follow her in-laws' advice and ignore the affair, but as the weeks wore on Steven become increasingly brazen—determined, Nancy felt, to rub her nose in his affair. If there had been any doubt that this was the case, it evaporated when he began telling Nancy to wrap up the dinners she had cooked so he could take them to his girlfriend. Finally, Nancy whipped off her apron and reached for her coat. "Fine, Steven, I'll go along," she said. "I'd really like to meet her."

To Nancy's amazement, Steven agreed. When Nancy walked into the tiny apartment, the other woman, completely unflustered, politely offered her a drink. Nancy only allowed herself to cry once she was behind the wheel of her car and driving home. What she somehow had tricked herself into believing would be a moment of righteous indignation had become one of utter, gut-wrenching humiliation.

The affair soon fizzled, but it no longer mattered. The marriage was over.

By mutual agreement, Steven would be the one to file for divorce—only because Nancy could not afford the legal fees. She would not contest it, nor would she ask for alimony or a property settlement. Nancy just wanted out.

Steven testified as follows:

> The problem with our marriage began approximately two years ago, when suddenly it seemed that nothing I did satisfied my wife. She constantly criticized me, the way I dressed, my friends, relatives, just everything. Often her criticism was vicious in nature and was performed in front of friends and relatives. This was extremely humiliating and embarrassing to me, and when I would ask my wife to please stop criticizing me in front of friends, she would go into fits of rage, yelling and swearing at me. She used extremely vile language against me—"son-of-a-bitch," "fucking asshole," "bastard." Often, after her fits of rage, she would give me the "silent treatment" and this would last for days on end.
>
> During the last year of our marriage my wife refused to do anything with me. I would ask her to go places,

to dinner, to parties, and she would just simply refuse. She told me that she couldn't stand me anymore, and didn't want to be married.

Although we did not need the money, she got a job and when I asked her why she was working she told me simply to "get away from me." During the last six months of our marriage before our separation, she completely refused to have marital relations with me, again stating that she simply couldn't stand me.

Also during the last few months before our separation my wife began staying out until the early hours of the morning, and when I would ask her where she had been she would give me no explanation. She would simply say that it was none of my business, and she really did not consider herself married anymore. . . .

Q. Will you tell the Court what effect this treatment had upon you?

A. I became nervous and upset to such a degree as to render my condition intolerable and my life burdensome.

Q. Has your condition improved since the date of separation?

A. Yes.

Q. What did you do to deserve this treatment and what did you do to make this marriage a success?

A. I did nothing to deserve this treatment, and I did everything in my power to make the marriage a success. I repeatedly forgave my wife for her actions and tried to reason with her and work out our problems. She simply refused to discuss them and all my efforts were to no avail.

Q. Who witnessed these events?

A. Our friends and relatives.

Q. Are these people available to corroborate your testimony?

A. No. These people have refused to become involved in my marital problems in any way.

Q. Who is paying the costs of this divorce action?

A. I am.

Amber leaves blanketed the front yard of 1510 Ridge Road, and Nancy felt a strange twinge of nostalgia as she rubbed her hands together against the November chill. She had come to pack her memories into cardboard boxes and haul them away. Steven was at his parents' house, and no sooner did he tell them that Nancy was across the street gathering up her belongings than Margaret and Edward hurried over—not to say goodbye, not even to gloat. They were there to make certain Nancy would not be taking anything that did not belong to her.

After Nancy and the Bensons finished dividing up the wedding presents, a friend helped Nancy load up a rented truck. As they pulled away, Nancy looked at Margaret standing alone in her driveway, arms folded across her chest, smiling victoriously. It was the last Nancy would ever see of her.

Mike Minney had offered Nancy a job as a secretary in his law office. Once she was on her feet, she would be free to pursue a childhood dream, working with farm animals as a veterinary nurse.

◆ ◆ ◆

Enter Debra Franks Larsen. It was on one of his increasingly frequent and lengthy stays in Wisconsin that Steven first encountered the buxom young tobacco sorter at the Lancaster Leaf plant there. Debbie, the comely blond daughter of a dairy farmer, moved in with Steven across

53

from Margaret and Benny just three months after Nancy's departure from the scene—despite the fact that Debbie was still very much married to someone else. A quick Dominican Republic divorce would prove a neat solution to that nettlesome problem, and Steve and Debbie marched to the altar June 7, 1980. Margaret was about to discover that she had met her match.

Chapter 10

The smoker's cough to which Benny's wife and children had become so accustomed was now more frequent and more severe. Visitors to the Benson house shifted uneasily in their seats as Benny, Scotch on the rocks in one hand and smoldering cigarette in the other, would struggle for as long as a full minute to regain his breath. Inevitably, a spot turned up on an X-ray of Benny's lungs. He was diagnosed as having lung cancer so advanced that it was doubtful he would live out the year.

Ever the businessman, Benny moved to consolidate his holdings, selling off, at a 110 percent profit, the house across the street, which they had purchased for Steven and Nancy, and another house they had bought on Ridge Road not long after they bought Steven's (both went for $156,000). He held on to the estate he owned in the ritzy Port Royal enclave of Naples, Florida; this was, after all, the dream house to which he and Margaret had planned to retire. His wife clearly loved the place, and perhaps there, Benny reasoned, she could make a new and happy life for herself, alone. Benny paid a visit to the red-brick warehouse in Lancaster that he had bought for the sole purpose of storing the family junk (Margaret had an aversion to throwing anything away) and his beloved antique cars. Inside, he walked past the accumulation of thirty years—patio furniture, lawn mowers, trunks full of clothing—to the 1929 Stutz Bearcat, the Lincoln, the vintage Jag. All in all, there were a dozen classic autos in varying states of disrepair, each waiting to be restored. The older models had not been in running order for years, and Benny knew he would never drive them again, but Margaret, he was confident, would see to it that they were cared for.

Benny sat down with his lawyer in early October and prepared a new will. He bequeathed all his personal property—including the houses and the cars—to his wife. The remaining $1.1 million of his estate was put in a trust for Margaret and the children. (Most of the couple's ten-million-dollar fortune, derived from Margaret's share of the Lancaster Leaf enterprise, was in his wife's name.) The will stressed that the trust would be shared by children "both natural and adopted," removing any doubt as to Scott's right to share equally with Carol Lynn and Steven in Benny's estate. One month later, at 11:05 on the night of November 5, Edward Benson died at Lancaster's St. Joseph Hospital, with his family at his bedside. He was sixty years old.

Nancy Benson (she had decided to keep her married name) called Steven to tell him how deeply sorry she was. She had always respected her father-in-law despite all that had transpired between her and the family. There was a long silence before Steven thanked her. As she hung up

the phone, she felt more sympathy for Steven than she
had expected to. The man whose early indifference had
caused his only son such pain was dead. What went with
Edward Benson was one final chance for Steven to earn
from his father the love he felt he had always been denied.
Perhaps better than Steven himself—probably more than
any of the other Bensons—Nancy felt she understood this.
And she grieved for Steven.

◆ ◆ ◆

The quiet eye of the family storm was gone, leaving behind nothing but the maelstrom. If there was any doubt
that Benny had been a stabilizing force for his wife and
children, that vanished with his death. Margaret now held
the all-important purse strings, and though she was or-
ganized to a fault, it was clear to everyone—particularly
to Steven and Scott—that she was no match for their father
when it came to money matters. Both young men were
eager to take advantage of the situation.

Like most other events that touched on the family, Edward Benson's death was an occasion for bitter fighting—
this time without the benefit of Father's somewhat calming
presence. Even before Benny's arrival on the embalmer's
table, his brood was squabbling again—this time over the
price and the design of his crypt. They settled on a stark
granite mausoleum near the front entrance to Lancaster's
Woodward Hill Cemetery, where President James Buchanan is also buried. The Benson-Hitchcock tomb, which
resembles a bunker as Frank Lloyd Wright might have
designed it, has a stained-glass window, ornate bronze
doors and room inside for eight. Edward Benson became

the tomb's first inhabitant on November 9, 1980. He would not be alone for long.

With Edward Benson gone, the management of Lancaster Leaf no longer felt obliged to keep Steven on the payroll. What they had not counted on, however, was that his father's passing had had a singularly liberating effect on Steven. At long last out of his father's shadow, out from under his control, he waited a respectable six weeks after the funeral to resign from Lancaster Leaf. Nor was Steven blind to the resentment harbored by his co-workers at Lancaster Leaf. So long as he was the boss's son, they had had little choice but to stand aside and watch Steven be groomed as heir apparent. Steven was still the founder's grandson, but he knew that without his father at the helm there was little chance that he'd make it to the top. And at the top was where Steven felt he deserved to be. Benny's longtime lieutenant and successor as president, Claude Martin, had always known that Steven was frustrated by the constant comparisons to his father, that he wanted to do something he could take full credit for, something he had accomplished on his own.

Steven wished, too, to show his mother that he was worthy of her respect. For her part, Margaret, a single woman for the first time in thirty-five years, felt cast adrift in a sea of financial sharks. Everyone—accountants, lawyers, bankers and architects—now circled the wreckage of her personal life, and she needed the love and support of her eldest son to fend them off. If it meant financing some of Steven's schemes, Margaret now seemed willing to take the chance.

Steven wasted no time plunging into an ambitious new project. On January 5, 1981—two months after Edward Benson's death—Steven set up a company to compete directly with the firm his grandfather had founded and his father had run for more than twenty years. Incorporated as the grandiose-sounding United International Industries, Inc., Steve's new enterprise was first and foremost intended to be a worldwide trader in tobacco. Before he had bought or sold so much as one leaf, Steve had ordered pencils and pens and calenders and business cards emblazoned with the United International Industries, Inc., logo, and set up a direct telex link with traders in the Philippines. But it soon became clear that United International Industries, Inc., could not woo so much as a single customer—international or otherwise—from Lancaster Leaf. Even in death, Father was winning again.

Chapter 11

"Hey, come look at this!" someone hollered to the shirtless worker on the roof of the house at 1515 Ridge Road. "Somebody shot the President!" Tom Schelling clambered down the ladder and into the living room, where the household staff and assorted construction men hired by Margaret Benson to complete the remodeling had gathered around the television set. For the next hour, they watched the tape of the incredible scene replayed again and again—a smiling Ronald Reagan waving to the crowd as he leaves the Washington Hilton, the stunned look as a shot rings out and secret service men push him into his waiting limousine, the camera finally coming to rest on the pathetic sight of presidential press secretary James Brady face down on the pavement, a bullet through his brain.

Like tens of millions of others, Tom Schelling shook his head in amazement and, reassured that the President was not fatally injured, returned to his work. There was certainly enough to do. Even though she was now spend-

ing nearly all her time down in Florida, Margaret insisted
that remodeling continue on the Lancaster house. She had
ordered Steven to make sure that repairs were made on
the roof, that a new skylight was installed above the
kitchen, that an outside porch area was screened in.

The shooting of the President, if totally unrelated to
the strange incident Schelling was about to witness,
served to fix the date—March 30, 1981—in his mind. He
was working on the skylight in the midday sun—already
surprisingly hot for early spring—when he heard the back
door slam. He turned to see Steven walking through the
pool area toward the gate surrounding the tennis courts.
He carried copper tubing with antenna-thin wires curling
out of the top. Schelling shrugged and went back to hammering. Less than a minute later, it happened—three explosions in rapid succession, each louder than a half stick
of dynamite. Once again, Schelling hurriedly jumped
down off the ladder.

What he saw when he got to the ground made him
shudder: Steven standing by the tennis courts, holding a
small black box in his hand. The box was about the size
of a garage door opener, and it had a red button and a
white button, each with a matching light. Steven stood
there, with his finger still pressing down on the red button, grinning broadly as smoke rose from the surface of
the courts.

Even with his father out of the picture once and for all,
Steven had been unable to make a go of his own business;
the stillborn United International Industries was proof
enough of that. Nothing he did was enough to please Margaret, or Debra. But for this brief moment, at least, Steven
could blow his troubles to kingdom come—at least sym-
bolically—simply by pushing a little red button. Tom

Schelling climbed back up the ladder, shaking his head in disbelief. He remembered the day Steven forgot to bring his gym clothes and stood there on the football field in his underwear, sobbing.

Chapter 12

The news in May of 1981 that Debra was pregnant brought the rosy tint back to Steven's perception of reality. Margaret, however, was no fonder of Debbie than she had been of Nancy. In fact, Debbie had given notice early on that she would be a formidable opponent in any battles for Steve's loyalty, if not for his affections. Steven's second wife had made it clear at the outset that she—and not Mother—would be the dominant female in Steven's life. Still, the fact that she was expecting forced Margaret to look at her daughter-in-law in a new light. She would, after all, be the mother of Benny's grandchild. Margaret's feelings toward Steven's second wife seemed to soften. The pregnancy brought mother and son, close since Benny's death, even closer.

Flush with the promise of yet another chance to carve out (with Mother's help, of course) a successful future on his own terms, Steven endeavored to find a property suitable for his new family. He found it in Norwood, a historic seventeen-acre horse farm built by artist Lloyd Mifflin, which overlooked the town of Columbia some fifteen miles west of Lancaster. Clinging to the side of a hill opposite the Windswept Riding Stables and surrounded by pines, oaks and elms, the two-story mansion itself was a quirky architectural concoction featuring a pink stone facade, black shutters, an overhanging roof and a wraparound porch. There was a columned portico in the rear, leading out to a brick courtyard and outbuildings beyond. A white clapboard wing off the main house was topped with a copper cupola. The grounds had not been tended and the exterior of the main house had gone slightly to seed, giving Norwood the appearance of a once-stately turn-of-the-century manor whose present owners, having inherited it from an eccentric uncle, could no longer afford the upkeep. Once he laid eyes on Norwood, however, Steve could see the possibilities. Scarcely a week after his first sight of the property, he and Debbie signed a sales agreement to purchase Norwood from James Blaxland for $240,000. Steve told Blaxland he intended to convert much of the estate to a housing tract, subdividing it into a dozen or so building lots.

He turned to Margaret for the five-figure down payment. Mother was livid, lighting into Steven for his irresponsible, spendthrift ways. Once Steve explained his plan to turn a handsome profit on the deal by subdividing Norwood, Margaret grudgingly went ahead and signed the check.

That summer, Steve was relieved to see Debbie take her place as chatelaine of Norwood. For the moment, at least, she would be sufficiently occupied with furnishing the twenty-two-room house and preparing for the birth of their child. But the plan to make millions by carving up the seventeen acres for a pricey subdivision never materialized. Typically, Steve had failed to consider that nearly all the subdividable acreage was at a severe slant—on the side of a hill too steep for construction. A complication he hadn't counted on, to be sure, but nothing to worry Mother over. Besides, Steve reasoned, she had other troubles with which to contend.

PART TWO

TROUBLE IN PARADISE

"My sister Margaret was enjoying life so much she got up at 6:30 A.M. just to have time for everything."
—JANET LEE MURPHY

"She was getting distraught in the thought that she was going broke. Mother had a terrible fear of nursing homes . . . and over this period she watched Steven go through money in terms of $50,000 and $150,000 . . ."
—CAROL LYNN BENSON KENDALL

Chapter 13

Life in Naples is a pastel haze—
a blur of white-hulled yachts, striped lawn tents and Izod-
shirted millionaires in pink-and-green madras jackets. The
place has its own texture, its own smell; the air is heavy
with the heady scent of gardenias, aloe and hard cash.
Ever since Charles Lindbergh landed his plane on Naples'
Fifth Avenue to escape the pomp and pretense of an already overbooked Palm Beach in the early 1930s, this small
Gulf Coast city has been a haven for Florida's Protestant
rich. The fortunes that have settled in Naples sprang
chiefly from the heartland—Indiana, Illinois, Ohio, Michigan and Pennsylvania—and from every imaginable enterprise from mining and manufacturing to banking, re-
tailing and the law. Not surprisingly, the influx of the
wealthy, most of them retirees, has meant a boom in those
professions designed to help affluent people hold on to
their money. Financial planners, stockbrokers, bankers,
accountants, trust officers and real estate sharpies of every

stripe make sizable fortunes of their own merely by tending these piles of gold; they thrive in the reflected glint.

The social landscape here is dotted with gilt-edged names like Vanderbilt and Rockefeller, but the average Naples millionaire (and it is estimated that perhaps as many as one fifth of the town's 110,000 residents fall into this category) can best be described as old nouveau riche—second- or third-generation money who spend with taste and confidence but don't let that get in the way of their fun. No gold chains and pinkie rings, thank you very much, but don't spare the Beluga caviar and the Dom Perignon. When Margaret and Edward Benson bought the house in Port Royal, former senator and Democratic presidential candidate George McGovern was building a health club in Naples. Novelist Robin Cook had escaped to a $600,000 condominium in Naples' Pelican Bay enclave and Robert Ludlum was spinning his Byzantine cloak-and-dagger yarns in a condo on pricey Gulf Shore Boulevard.

No neighborhood in Naples, however, is more exclusive—or expensive—than Port Royal. Mansard-roofed chateaus, sprawling haciendas and mansions fashioned after Japanese teahouses stand side by side with the angular contemporaries and the stucco-and-glass designs favored by the native Floridian. Royal palms, jonquils, bird-of-paradise and hibiscus grow here in abundance, tended by Cuban and Japanese gardeners bent on outdoing one another. Each house boasts a circular drive paved with coral stone or white seashells, and each backs onto a canal leading to the Gulf, giving Port Royal the general appearance of a cross between Venice and Beverly Hills.

By 1980, no house could be had at Port Royal for less than $500,000, and many fetched in the millions. Money was not the only criterion if you wanted to live here; until a civil suit resulted in a court order prohibiting such discrimination, the residents of Port Royal prided themselves on belonging to a restricted community where prospective home owners had to pass a background screening before permission to purchase property was granted.

Whatever skeletons were hanging in the Benson family closet apparently went undetected by Port Royal investigators. Edward and Margaret passed with flying colors, and proceeded to pay a half million dollars in cash for their white-walled, mansard-roofed residence at 1030 Galleon Drive. Benny spent only a few weeks in the house before his death, but it was time enough for him to see that living here amid the yachts and the palms made Margaret happy.

Her own happiness was not Margaret's only reason for wanting to relocate to Naples and Port Royal. Scott, now well into his teens, showed great promise as a tennis player, she was convinced of that, and there was no better place for him to hone his skills than here on Florida's west coast, regarded as one of the sport's premier training centers. If Scott's energies could only be channeled in the right direction, she thought, he could be another Connors, another McEnroe.

Scott certainly seemed to have the temperament for it. Headstrong and cocky, he was already living life in the fast lane by the time he graduated from high school at seventeen. After all, he had the looks and he had the seven-thousand-dollar *monthly* allowance Margaret doled out to him—enough money to keep himself and his friends well supplied with cocaine, marijuana and booze, though his chief addiction remained the "grocery store high" he got from sniffing nitrous oxide out of whipped cream cans. Scott had learned this nasty little trick back in the eighth grade, when he started snatching the whipped cream canisters from his mother's kitchen. By the time he was a sophomore in high school, Scott was buying whipped cream by the case from gourmet food stores, and then selling what he didn't use to his friends.

Margaret looked the other way, preferring instead to focus on Scott's budding talent as a professional tennis player. Toward that end, she hired the first of what would be a series of high-priced instructors—most of whom would wind up telling her that Scotty, while a good player, simply did not have the physical equipment to become a first-class competitor. No matter. Margaret was determined to make Scott a tennis pro, regardless of the cost. It was her mission in life. And if there was one thing Margaret knew, it was this: There is no problem in life so big that it can't be solved by money.

In the spring of 1981, it looked as if Margaret was about to be proved right. She had plunked down the ten-thousand-dollar fee to send Scotty to the Harry Hopkins International Training Camp at chic Bardmoor Country Club north of St. Petersburg, and early reports were good. Scotty's regimen: up at 6 A.M. to run five miles, then six hours of instruction and practice. The pace was demanding, and he seemed to have little time for his customary hell-raising. For the time being, he also managed to do without his daily jolt of laughing gas; he even managed to cut back on his pot consumption.

Margaret hadn't counted on Tracy. Scotty was doing laps at the Bardmoor pool when he spotted the tall, leggy, green-eyed stunner sunning herself in a blue bikini. Tracy Mullins was fourteen, and had started hanging around the country club only a week or so before. Scott asked her out.

Two weeks later, she quit school and moved in with Scott at his Bardmoor condo.

Tracy instantly took to playing house, cleaning up after her compulsively messy "husband," cooking his meals, doing the shopping. They called each other "Sweetheart" and "Honey," and one night Scott surprised her with a gold ring set with a quarter-carat diamond. She watched him practice, and he took her miniature golfing. For protection, Scott bought a Bouvier des Flandres and hired an expert to train him as an attack dog. Scott named him Buck.

Like everyone who loved him, Tracy found it necessary to overlook Scott's arrogant, sometimes violent behavior. There was, for example, the time she got caught between Scott and the police when he was barred from a Clearwater restaurant because he was drunk. Then there was the incident at a roller rink, a sort of singles hangout that also attracted more than its share of unsuspecting parents in search of ways to entertain young children. The rink's security guard watched in amazement as Scott appeared to deliberately careen into one woman from behind, sending her sprawling. When the guard ran up to throw him out, Scott insisted that it was an accident and refused to go. A hair-pulling match ensued before Scott finally left, yelling obscenities at the stunned crowd of skaters as he walked away.

Chapter 14

Margaret was worried. Worried that "they"—the bankers, the CPAs, the stockbrokers, the car dealers, everybody—were out to swindle her out of her millions. Worried that the children were wasting her money. Worried that, without Benny to protect her, she would wind up old and alone and penniless in a nursing home. She was almost sixty. She had to be sure that when the time came, she could afford to have a live-in nurse care for her in her declining years. Margaret repeatedly called up her daughter, Carol Lynn, now divorced and studying broadcast journalism and film in Boston, to voice her fears. At the rate everyone was going through her money, Margaret complained, it was only inevitable that she would soon find herself destitute. Carol Lynn tried to assuage her mother's fears. She called her "Little Miss Milquetoast." Even Margaret had to laugh.

Her fears, though extreme, had some basis in fact. Margaret had spent freely on her homes and her cars; two fire-engine-red Lotus turbos, for example, cost her even more than the Porsche—about fifty thousand dollars each. Then there was the private armada she had begun to build since her more or less permanent relocation in Florida: the thirty-six-foot yacht *Galleon Queen*, with its full-time captain and crew, her twenty-eight foot *Sea Ray* and the hundred-thousand-dollar cigarette racing boat she had promised Scotty.

What she spent, however, Margaret kept track of. She liked to tell friends that, before Benny's death, she didn't even know how to make out a check. But Margaret had always been a chronic list-maker and a meticulous record-keeper. Now she found herself waking up at 3 A.M., throwing on a robe and shuffling into the library of the Port Royal house to begin doing paperwork. Most of all, she kept a watchful eye on the balance of her Dean Witter Reynolds Active Assets Account, which generally fluctuated between four and five million dollars and thus accounted for around 40 percent of her ten-million-dollar total estate. Margaret had also begun keeping a balance sheet on the children, toting up the score in columns marked Loans and Accounts Receivable. By July 9, 1985, Margaret Benson's accounts would show that she was still owed $111,560.33 by Carol Lynn, $218,171.69 by Scott and $263,856.30 by Steven.

For all the burning of midnight oil, Margaret fell behind. She held on to receipts for every expense over a dollar, but bills went unpaid. She requested extensions to pay her quarterly estimated taxes. She needed help, and in July of 1981 asked her Lancaster broker to recommend an accountant who could help unravel her problems with Pennsylvania and Florida state income taxes. The broker recommended a young Philadelphia CPA and Temple University Law School alumnus named Wayne Kerr.

When he came to her house in Lancaster, Margaret was startled by Wayne Kerr's resemblance to her son Steven. Like Steve, Kerr was a bear of a man—well over six feet tall, he tipped the scales at perhaps 250 pounds. He wore wrinkled suits, thick glasses and a thin mustache. He sweated profusely, gobbled down Twinkies and had a fatal weakness for lasagna. Kerr had a peculiar habit of wheezing through his mouth, which gave his speech an unsettling quality similar to that of a deep-sea diver talking to the surface between intakes of oxygen. Or someone struggling to reach the top of Mount Everest. When he became excited, a state in which Kerr often found himself, it seemed inevitable that he was prone to hyperventilation. On occasions like this, he more closely resembled an agitated Oliver Hardy.

The physical resemblance, it turned out, was not Kerr's only link to Steve. Hershey-born Kerr, the son of a high-ranking thirty-five-year veteran of the Pennsylvania state police force, had moved to Lancaster when he was thirteen. It was then, while attending Lancaster Township Junior High School, that he first heard of Benson, when a teacher mistook him for Steve. Later, at McCaskey High, Kerr sat next to Nancy Ferguson in French 3. He had a crush on her, but it was Steve who pulled up to the front of the school each day in his red Mercedes to give Nancy a lift home. Despite this, Wayne Kerr and Steve Benson never met, never spoke.

That changed in November of 1981, when Kerr, already accustomed to being summoned by Margaret at a moment's notice, was called to 1515 Ridge Road. Margaret had flown up to Lancaster from Naples to iron out the taxes on some of her real estate, and Steve was standing in the living room when Kerr walked in. Both sensing they were long destined to become friends, Wayne and Steve hit it off immediately. Wayne noted that both were Cancers, and suggested that that was why they seemed to share much the same temperament. Soon Steve was staying over at Wayne's house in Philly, where they would hit the local nightspots and then discuss Steve's latest business ideas well into the early-morning hours. It became clear straightaway to Wayne that Steve was creative; it would take him a little longer to realize that Margaret's eldest son lacked the resolve and the practical know-how to turn his dreams into realities.

Kerr, for his part, had his hands full with Margaret. Despite her constant demands and her anxiety attacks, which often triggered angry tirades, Kerr had developed a fondness for her. She seemed to him a warm, caring woman who perhaps too frequently let her money worries get out of hand. He promised Margaret that he would be her "watchdog," her ample "buffer zone" against the army of vampires presumably out to bleed her dry.

◆ ◆ ◆

Charlotte Hitchcock died in September 1981, leaving 179,200 shares of Universal Leaf stock, valued at $4.5 million—one third of Hitchcock's 25 percent controlling interest in the family holding company—to Harry and in trust to the grandchildren. The income to Carol Lynn, Steven and Scott would be around thirty thousand dollars a year—nowhere near enough to support any of them in the style to which each had become accustomed.

It began to drizzle as Charlotte was laid to rest next to Edward Benson in the family crypt. At least, Harry would later thank God, she was spared the knowledge of horrors to come.

Chapter 15

On December 28, 1981, Debra gave premature birth to twins—Christopher Logan and Victoria Elizabeth—at Hershey Hospital. The babies remained at the hospital for the first six weeks of their lives, until they were strong enough to go home to Norwood in February. The marriage, already strained by Margaret's constant demands on Steven, now began to come apart at the seams, in part over what role—if any—Grandmother was to play in the lives of Christopher and Victoria.

Debra, like Nancy before her, was frustrated by Steven's refusal to snip the apron strings that tied him to Mother. When Margaret snapped her fingers, Steven still jumped—whether it was to keep tabs on the continuous parade of carpenters and workmen who labored on Margaret's never-ending construction projects or to update the security system that protected the Lancaster estate. Margaret was summoning him down to Naples so often to help her iron out financial problems both real and imagined that Steven put a down payment on a modest three-bedroom house there.

The mother versus daughter-in-law wars were not quite so lopsided this time around. Where Nancy had been powerless to bring about a change in either Steven or his family, the grandchildren gave Debra leverage. When Margaret ignored Debra's orders not to spoil the kids and arrived with a vanload of toys, Debbie forbade Margaret to see them at all, and laid down her own set of rules governing Steven's availability. Margaret was not to call Steven at home under any circumstances, only at the office or on his car phone. Debra enforced the rule with gusto, slamming the receiver down the instant she heard Margaret's voice.

Margaret was crushed, particularly over being barred from seeing Christopher and Victoria. But she still had the upper hand; Steven needed her money to make the payments on Norwood and to bankroll his real estate ventures. Less than a month after she brought the twins home from the hospital, Debbie packed them up and fled to her parents' farm in Westby, Wisconsin.

The separation lasted only a few weeks; Debbie decided that perhaps they might be able to start afresh in Florida—but only if Margaret would abide by the rules not to bother Steven at home and not to have any contact with the children. The experiment did not work. In July, Debbie returned to Wisconsin with Christopher and Victoria in tow. By September, she and Steven were officially separated, and not long after, Debbie instructed her attorneys to file divorce papers in Lancaster County's Court of Common Pleas, claiming that the marriage was "irretrievably broken" and that Steven's behavior had "rendered her condition intolerable and life burdensome." The papers also stated that Debra, lacking "sufficient property to provide for her reasonable means and . . . unable to support herself through appropriate employment," was entitled to alimony and child support.

At Norwood, a heavy layer of dust coated the mahogany furniture and weeds choked the lawn. With Steven now spending virtually all his time in Florida and Debbie pressing her divorce case from Wisconsin, Steven's grand plans again went up in smoke. Property taxes went unpaid, and by June, Steve, who had poured $60,000 into his white elephant, stopped meeting the $1,755 monthly mortgage payments altogether. In November, Jim Blaxland repossessed Norwood. It had been precisely one year since Edward Benson's death.

Chapter 16

Scotty had expected this reaction. Mother was furious. She had stood by while Tracy took up residence with him in Naples, had looked the other way when he wrecked a car or when nefarious-looking characters rang the doorbell in the middle of the night to exchange money and God-knew-what. Now he was telling her that he had taken Tracy to the Planned Parenthood office in Naples and that they had confirmed what Tracy had suspected: she was pregnant.

And now Margaret sneered. A gold digger, that's all she really was—out to snare a rich kid. He was only nineteen. This would ruin his tennis career. Besides, how could he even be sure the child was his? Margaret asked. Scott reacted predictably. He screamed that he loved Tracy and that she loved him. Then he grabbed Margaret by the shoulders and shook her menacingly. She was not, Scott told his mother, going to run his life anymore. Margaret's reply was straightforward: If he chose to remain with Tracy and the baby, Mother would cut off his funds and disinherit him. That simple. And, she gently reminded him, Mother was not one for making idle threats.

The next day, when Scott told her to get an abortion or leave, Tracy refused. She knew this was all his mother's doing, and pleaded with Scott to at long last break free from Margaret's influence. She told him they were already married, in spirit anyway, and if they could just get away from Margaret they could live a normal family life—something he had never known. Scott stormed off, leaving Margaret free to kick Tracy Mullins out of her house and out of Scott's life. Tracy returned to her parents' home in Hobart, Indiana, and gave birth to a daughter, Shelby Nicole, in July of 1983. The next month, unable to break through the wall Margaret had thrown up around Scott, she filed a paternity suit. Responding to the suit, Scott signed a lengthy, lawyer-drafted letter in which he credited his mother with setting him straight: "She, not being blinded by the forces of sexuality, very quickly perceived the true character of Tracy Mullins and was much opposed to my seeing her."

Margaret rewarded Scott with his own place in Clearwater, and he wasted no time replacing Tracy with Kimberly Beegle, a local girl he had met at a popular Naples bar called Andy's. Every inch a golden Florida girl, Kim was small—just a little over five feet tall—buxom, blue-eyed, blond and seventeen. She had an infectious laugh and, like Tracy, was totally devoted to Scott. Scott told her that if she dropped out of school and quit her job as a waitress, he'd keep her in a style to which she had not yet become accustomed. For starters, he promised to buy her a new outfit every week—a promise he would keep until the day he died.

Chapter 17

Steven knew there were still millions to be made developing commercial and residential property in and around Naples, which federal census records were showing as the fastest-growing city in America. Of course, Steven wasn't much for studying, and might never have passed the more difficult Pennsylvania real estate exam. But the Florida test was a breeze, and on March 31, 1983, Tallahassee mailed Steven the license that would at last enable him to pursue the real estate career he had put on hold back in Lancaster. From her vantage point in Wisconsin, Debra allowed herself to believe that Steven was for once taking some practical steps toward independence. She took the chance and moved in with Steven yet again. Reconciled—this time, Debra prayed, for good—she promptly became pregnant with their third child.

Steven felt recharged. Why stop at real estate? He sat down alone at the kitchen table and began to scribble the names of companies that could provide the services southwest Florida would be hungering for in the coming years. By the time he had finished, he had come up with no fewer than eleven companies—all under the "Meridian" umbrella: Meridian Real Estate, of course, but also Meridian Construction, Meridian Security Network, Meridian Technologies, Meridian Property Management, Meridian Marketing, Meridian Legal Services, Meridian Design and Engineering, Meridian Financial Services, Meridian Leasing and Meridian Condominiums.

The cornerstone of this mini empire was to be Meridian Security, basically a burglar- and fire-alarm business that would cater to the security needs of Naples' wealthier home owners as well as those of local companies. The market was certainly there; gone were the days when residents could leave their homes with windows and doors wide open to allow in the cooling breezes off the gulf. And there was no doubt in anyone's mind that this was one area in which Steven's technical know-how was unsurpassed. It was Steven, after all, who oversaw the installation of all alarms and security devices for the family's homes and vehicles. Even Harry Hitchcock agreed that if Steven was to have a shot at success, this was an area tailor-made for his particular talents. "Electronics is something he knows about," Harry told his daughter. "It's something he is competent to do."

Margaret agreed to bankroll Meridian. She would be listed as chairman of the board and would keep a tight rein on the finances, but Steven would have a free hand in the day-to-day running of the business. True to form, Steven ordered up expensive embossed business cards, a new beeper and a full-page ad in the Naples Yellow Pages, announcing that Meridian Security would provide "proven, reliable, state-of-the-art technology for residential, commercial, industrial, financial, agricultural, institutional, marine, aircraft, and vehicles." The various security measures offered: PRESENCE DETECTION—STRESS, SEISMIC, PROXIMITY; MOTION DETECTION—INFRARED, MICROWAVE, SONIC; TOUCH SENSE CAPACITANCE and OUTDOOR BEAMS AND SENSORS." The ad, twice as big and several times more costly than the ads of any of Meridian's more established competitors, proclaimed the opening of Meridian offices in "Ft. Myers and other cities" and invited prospective clients to "call for free survey or visit our showrooms." In truth, there was only one base of operations: a cramped trailer in an East Naples industrial park.

Chapter 18

September 12, 1983. Scott pounded down Galleon Drive and into the home stretch of his customary early-morning five-mile run. Sweating freely, he went straight to his bedroom, threw open the closet door, placed the face mask over his nose and mouth, turned on the valve leading to the green five-foot-high tank filled with nitrous oxide and breathed deeply. He needed to inhale much larger amounts of laughing gas now to get high; he had built up a tolerance since he first started sniffing the gas from the nozzles of whipped cream canisters, and the old grocery store high just didn't do the trick anymore. Not even scuba tanks were large enough to hold the quantities he required; he managed to obtain these huge cans from his auto mechanic on the pretext of using the nitrous oxide to soup up the Lotuses.

Scott sat at the edge of the bed for a moment, then lay back on the rumpled sheets to let that floating feeling take over again.

Just as she had done every morning since she took the

job as Margaret Benson's personal secretary several months before, Joyce Quinn let herself in the front door at precisely eight-thirty. The pretty, petite brunette headed straight for the library, where she usually began her work routine by calling the answering service to check for messages. She could hear Scott's girlfriend, Kim, in the kitchen, whipping up his breakfast.

The library at 1030 Galleon Drive was a large rectangular room. Margaret's oversized, meticulously kept desk squatted beneath the high windows that faced the front of the house. Parallel to the desk was an even larger wooden worktable, piled high with financial records, bills and correspondence. At the opposite end of the room, by the door that led from the library to a hallway and the adjacent bedrooms, was a Xerox machine.

Before Quinn could pick up the telephone to call the answering service this morning, Margaret appeared. She beckoned her secretary into the living room. "Look at this," Margaret said, shaking her head in disgust and pointing to a faint yellow-beige spot on the white living room rug. "That damned dog of Scott's made a mess and now the carpet is ruined. I've scrubbed and scrubbed and still can't get the stain out." Margaret had, in fact, banned Buck from the house; she could not tolerate the animal's habits of shedding all over her furniture, drinking out of the toilets and barking whenever a car drove by the house. Ironically, it was Margaret who had let Buck into the house on this occasion, though that fact did nothing to mollify her.

Margaret and her secretary went back into the library, and while Quinn began feeding papers into the copying machine, she listened to Margaret continue her harangue. "That was an expensive rug, and now it is completely ruined. I've told Scott again and again. I've just about had it with that filthy animal of his. I'm not going to put up with this. . . ."

A strange moaning sound began to come from the direction of the bedrooms, down the hallway just opposite Quinn as she stood there, still feeding papers into the copier. Then, within an instant, the moaning became weird, hysterical fun-house laughter. At first, Quinn thought someone was kidding. She prayed someone was kidding.

Suddenly, Scott flung open his door and ran into the library. Quinn froze. The Xerox machine was still humming. All color had drained from Margaret's face, though the traces of her contempt remained. Quinn stared on in wide-eyed wonder, her hands still feeding paper into the machine, robotlike. The veins in Scott's neck and forehead were engorged with rage.

"*Leave my dog alone*," he shouted at Margaret. "Can you understand that? He is an attack dog, Mother. *An attack dog.* And I can have him kill you anytime I want. If you ever do this again, I will have him kill you. I will have him tear you to pieces. Tear you to pieces, Mother . . ."

Margaret said nothing. Instead, she picked up the Sony tape recorder from the desk and turned it on to record Scott's threats.

Scott seemed unfazed. "Mother, I don't have to do anything. I give you all the respect you deserve."

"What do you mean by that, Scott? *Scott?*" Margaret, looking directly into those dilated pupils, knew what she was dealing with here.

"Say it over—'The dog is Scott Benson's. The dog is Scott Benson's.' " He pulled the recorder closer. "Say it right into the tape. I'm going to trap you, Mother. That's why I wanted Joyce here, because she's just another character witness. She works for you. Hear that, Mother, Joyce was here when you said that, because she is a character witness and she will *expect to be in court*. Because this is a serious situation. Because the dog *is not yours*, and you listen when I tell you. . . . Just because it's your house, it doesn't mean you do what you want with *my dog*. Can you understand that? Huh? Do you? *Do you?*"

Scott snatched the recorder out of Margaret's grasp as she backed away, toward the worktable. "Get your hands off—" she screamed in the instant before he smashed the recorder full force against the edge of the table, sending pieces of plastic and metal flying. Then Scott, his fury mounting, grabbed Margaret by the shoulders and shook her hard. She became hysterical. "Joyce, call the police. Call the police!" Quinn hesitated. Margaret had a penchant for changing her mind, and Quinn was not eager to explain to the police that it had all been just a little misunderstanding. But this time, even after Scott had stormed back into his room, Quinn could tell from the look of terror in Margaret's eyes that she should go ahead and make the call.

Afterward, Quinn walked outside, to the edge of the canal behind the house, and took a deep breath to steady herself. It was an idyllic scene: Sailboats and cabin cruisers named after the owners' grandchildren were tied to private docks, palms waved in the September breeze. She shook her head and returned to the front of the house to wait for the Naples police. By the time the squad car pulled up, ten minutes later, Margaret had joined her, still shaking. Able only to give her name, Margaret left it up to her secretary to describe the situation to the officers.

"Any weapons?" asked Detective William Lanzisera.

89

When Quinn assured him that there weren't any guns in the house, the police told Margaret what she had already known: Under Florida's Baker Act, a minor who is deemed suicidal, homicidal or incompetent to care for himself or herself can be hospitalized involuntarily for psychiatric evaluation. It was one of the state's better-known mental health statutes, designed primarily for handling people under the influence of drugs or alcohol, and it was one Margaret had thought of using many times before. Lanzisera instructed the two women to move to the opposite side of the U-shaped driveway while the officers went in through the front door to get Scott.

Inside Scott's bedroom, the two detectives found two empty tanks that had once contained laughing gas. Scott, eyes glassy and face flushed, wasn't about to be thrown out by Margaret. "Fuck!" he yelled. "You can't do this. My mother's crazy!" Before he could make a break for it, Scott was wrestled to the floor and handcuffed. Outside, standing on the far side of the driveway, Margaret and Quinn could hear the muffled sounds of the struggle inside. By now, a number of the neighbors, their gardeners and their maids had gathered on the lawns and on the sidewalk to watch the commotion. Others caught the show from inside their homes. As he was being hauled to the waiting car, Scott pleaded with his mother to call off the police. "Oh, Mother, please help me," he begged. "Look what they're doing to me. Oh, please . . . *Mother!*" Margaret just stood there, still trembling. Back inside the library, Quinn found the microcassette amid the shattered remains of the tape recorder, placed it in a plain white envelope, dated the envelope and sealed it. The next time Quinn heard the tape, she would be listening to voices from the grave.

Chapter 19

The Scott Benson Dr. José Lombillo met that day in the psychiatric ward at Naples Community Hospital seemed far short of menacing. He squirmed in his seat, shooting to his feet occasionally to pace the floor. He was tense, impatient, confused, aware of the fact that policemen had brought him to the hospital but unable to remember what had gone on before. And he was afraid. Sweat beading on his forehead and his hands shaking, Scott confessed his anxieties to Lombillo. He was scared that he was losing his memory. Scared he was losing his ability to concentrate, perhaps losing his mind. Even his tennis was suffering.

Lombillo listened to the familiar litany: In middle school, when he was twelve years old, Scott began smoking pot, then dropping acid, popping speed; and in high school, he snorted cocaine. Lombillo had encountered others, mostly young boys, hooked on nitrous oxide sniffed from aerosol cans, though the sheer magnitude of Scott's consumption—usually accompanied by pot, booze, or both—amazed the psychiatrist. Scott took a blast not once every night before bed, but sometimes several times a day; he sometimes toted a scuba tank full of the stuff with him in his car.

An electroencephalogram and a CAT scan showed no permanent neurological damage, though a urinalysis revealed a discernible amount of marijuana residue in Scott's system. Lombillo also discovered that Scott suffered from a mild case of anemia, and prescribed a series of vitamin B_{12} shots during the patient's stay. But Scott's mood swings and his tirades led to one incontrovertible diagnosis: organic brain syndrome, a temporary change in brain chemistry induced by drugs.

If none of the clinical facts seemed particularly out of the ordinary, the family scenario that had set the stage for such bizarre behavior struck Lombillo as unique. Here was someone who at eighteen had had his own condo at Bardmoor, who was accustomed to driving fifty-thousand-dollar sports cars, who brought his underaged girlfriends home to live with him. He was the quintessential spoiled brat, a kid with no sense of the value of money, yet as addicted to spending it as he was to inhaling laughing gas. It would not have surprised the psychiatrist had he learned that in just two years, Margaret had lavished in the neighborhood of $250,000 on the boy.

His father had always controlled the family finances, Scott told Lombillo. Edward Benson was the head of a huge company, for Christ sake. He knew what he was doing. But Mother . . . What in the hell did she know about handling money? Why should she have anything to say about how much money Scott spent? She had sold stock that was held in trust in his name, saying it was to settle his debts. Scott wanted the proceeds from the sale released to him, but his usual ploy of throwing a tantrum just wasn't having the desired results. Scott was willing to sue his mother if that's what it was going to take. He had hired a New York lawyer to do just that.

On this as well as other matters, Lombillo learned from Scott in their sessions at the hospital and during treatment afterward, Scott had sought advice from his big brother. Scott described Steven as quiet, distant, intellectual, introspective—not a talker. It was as if Steven was floating above the turmoil on a cloud of his own. He seemed, Lombillo judged from Scott's biased depiction, to have a stabilizing, even calming effect on the family. Steven had even found himself caught once or twice in the middle of one of Scott's battles with Carol Lynn. Scott and she fought constantly, sometimes even coming to blows, over everything from Scott's treatment of Margaret to what Carol Lynn called Scott's "sleazo" girlfriends. Lombillo marveled that Carol Lynn, a woman approaching forty, and her brother were like two teenagers constantly at each other's throats. Doubtless he would have found their relationship even more curious had he known the whole truth—that Carol Lynn was Scott's mother.

On September 20, nine days after he was admitted, Scott was released "symptom free" from Naples Community Hospital, a folder of magazine articles on overcoming drug dependency tucked under his arm. Dr. Lombillo had arranged with Scott's coach, Dick McNamara, to provide Scott with a daily regimen that left him little time to resume his past abuses. Scott had come to realize that he loved Margaret—that all she wanted was the best for him. Who else believed in his tennis career, such as it was, as much as Mother? But he also knew that living in the same house with her was probably not healthy for either

93

of them. Scott spoke of plans to put some distance between himself and his mother, to move away from Naples
and into an apartment of his own in Fort Myers, forty-five
minutes to the north. After his release, Scott would see
Lombillo on four separate occasions. The last was shortly
before Christmas. He was still living with Margaret.

Chapter 20

The "Incident," as it was politely being referred to, had not gone unnoticed by the powers that be in Port Royal. They wanted Margaret and Scott out, and Port Royal's deed restrictions prohibiting such unseemly goings-on gave them the legal clout to do it. The house on Galleon Drive, which of late had seemed a little cramped and commonplace to Margaret anyway, was snapped up almost as soon as it went on the market, for $650,000, but the new owners had to move in in a matter of five weeks. Margaret cast about for a place to live and came upon it ten miles to the north, in another haven for the rich, called Quail Creek.

Steven approved. Before even setting foot in Quail Creek, a visitor first had to get past a uniformed guard at the entry gate. Behind the gate was a new community carved out of a patch of wilderness adjacent to the Corkscrew Swamp Sanctuary. Many of the houses that hugged Quail Creek's two Arthur Hills–designed championship golf courses were every bit as grand as those in Port

Royal—pink stucco villas; Alhambra-like designs with fountains, cobalt-blue tile roofs and Moorish archways; mini Monticellos; a smattering of mansard-roofed French colonials. The streets had names like Coco Plum Lane, Bald Cyprus Street and Pond Apple Drive. The crowning glory of Quail Creek was its huge, shake-roofed clubhouse with four private dining rooms, health club, pool and lighted tennis courts. Residents who plunked down anywhere from $400,000 to more than $1 million for a house had the option of joining the club for a mere $25,000 extra.

The house at 13002 White Violet Drive was one of Quail Creek's least pretentious—a one story, stucco-walled house in the Florida modern tradition, with sloping roof lines of orange tile, arched windows, skylights and a glassed-in lanai. But this was only to be a temporary residence, and the price—under $300,000—was right, so reasonable, in fact, that Margaret had plenty left over to buy the adjacent lot facing Butterfly Orchid Lane.

She had been resisting selling the house at 1515 Ridge Road in Lancaster for some time, filled as it was with memories of Boppa and raising her children and her life with Benny. But the time had come, and Margaret put her thirty-five-year-old Lancaster dream house on the market. The Lancaster *Intelligencer-Journal* ran a full-page story on the sale in its "Lifestyle" section on June 25, 1984. "What can you get in a $475,000 house?" the headline asked. "Well, almost anything you want." The accompanying photographs showed the formal dining room with its massive crystal chandelier, the kitchen's twin ovens, twin ranges and twin refrigerators, and the real estate agent posing on the arched wooden bridge over Margaret's carp pond.

For her part, Margaret was happy to immerse herself

in new projects. She still had to find the property on which she would build her permanent estate, the house where she intended to spend the rest of her life. But there was time to start enjoying life again. Generally shunning the cocktail circuit, Margaret made an exception now and then for the small group of Lancaster residents with winter homes in Naples, occasionally accepting their invitations to play bridge or go boating. But she had long ago given up the mindless whirl of coffee klatches and charity fashion shows that had filled her days in Lancaster back in the 1950s and '60s. Nor was she particularly interested in finding a husband; she had far too much money not to be suspicious of any suitor's motives. So Margaret swam, practiced her backhand and played hostess to her family. She still made an effort to travel north to visit Harry and her sister Janet, but now she was secure enough in her new home to reciprocate. Boppa and Janet began flying down to Naples every few months, and Margaret took special delight in taking them out on the *Galleon Queen*. "Daddy and I liked to come down because we had such a good time together," Janet would later recall. "Margaret was enjoying life so much that she got up at 6:30 A.M. just to have time for everything."

Carol Lynn also grew closer to her mother, taking every available opportunity to break away from her film studies in Boston—and the two teenage sons who had become something of a handful—and join Margaret in Naples. Now, Carol Lynn had come to realize, there was really only Mother to turn to. Her mother had become her best friend; there was an unspoken bond between them.

Not that an outsider would have seen it. The legendary battles they had sustained over the dinner table back in Lancaster were not forgotten, and neither mother nor daughter now shrank from an argument. Squabbling, often bitterly, was second nature to Margaret and Carol Lynn. (One guest at the Benson house in Lancaster recalled a pitched battle among the adults over what brand of cereal they were going to have for breakfast.) So to anyone who knew them it came as no surprise when they lit into one another over silly, inconsequential things. The color of drapes. Where to put a light fixture or a sofa. They *enjoyed* sparring, just as they enjoyed dining together at Naples' gulfside restaurants, checking out the local real estate, shopping for hours. One afternoon Margaret, whose taste ran to wraparound skirts and simple sundresses, decided it was time to jazz up her wardrobe with a few casual outfits and headed for her favorite boutique. The bill: twelve thousand dollars.

A favorite topic of conversation for mother and daughter was Steven. His business, much to Carol Lynn's amazement, seemed to be taking off. Steven had decided to pare the operation down from the original eleven Meridian companies to five, and it looked as if Meridian Security, the cornerstone of the little empire, had landed its share of lucrative contracts with home owners and businesses and was likely to turn a profit. But, Margaret told her daughter, the personal price was too high. Debra still forbade Margaret to call Steven at home or ever see the grandchildren. Little Natalie Nicole was almost a year old now, but Grandma was not permitted by Debra to send so much as a birthday card.

Carol Lynn was angry. Angry that Debra could be so rigid, and that her brother could be so weak. She picked up the phone and called Steven. How could he do this to Mother? Who had ever heard of not being permitted to see your own grandchildren? Be a man, for God's sake, and stand up to your wife. Steven took his usual tack: He listened for several minutes in total silence as his sister talked on. Then he slammed down the receiver.

Chapter 21

Scott looked in the rearview mirror, saw the flashing lights of the patrol car behind him and floored it.

Margaret was startled awake by the phone. For the sixth time in twenty months, Scott was picked up for speeding—only this time he had tried to outrun the cops in his Lotus. If anything, Scott seemed more reckless than ever. He had totaled the Datsun 280Z. He had driven the family's tan-and-brown GMC diesel right off Alligator Alley—the monotonous stretch of interstate that cuts straight through the Everglades—and into a swamp. Kim and Scott took snapshots of the pickup being pulled from the muck, water cascading out of the windows. They laughed, and from that point on, he had a new nickname: "Aquaman." Margaret was not amused. Towing and repair had cost her $3,077.51. And there was the matter of her pearls. Margaret was certain that one of Scott's girlfriends had pilfered them.

Margaret was not about to give up on Scott. She had helped all her children in the only way she knew how—with money—and she was determined to do the same for her youngest. Margaret had already spent a fortune for the best coaches and the best trainers—professionals she kept close tabs on and did not hesitate to berate if they failed to get results. She had thought it perfectly logical to buy sixteen tennis rackets for Scott before he was satisfied, and would have bought him sixteen more if she thought it would help his serve one iota.

Scott's commitment to tennis was at best erratic. He plunged into the part-time job he had at the local YMCA, giving kids pointers on the game, but he was still chronically late for his own practice sessions. He had also gotten over the unpleasantness of his brief stay in the psychiatric unit at Naples Community Hospital. The laughing gas was no longer flowing quite so freely, but Scott seemed to be drinking and toking up more than ever. Where Steven sought to impress with grandiose business schemes, Scott often sprang for enough cocaine to keep his pals high for an evening.

Edward Malone, a Naples roofer with the kind of WASP good looks and *Gentleman's Quarterly* wardrobe that made him look right at home in Scott's well-heeled brat pack, had first met Scott at a tournament in the summer of 1982 and became his frequent tennis partner. Late the next year, Malone watched as young Benson got up in the middle of a party at the ultra-chic Naples Racquet and Tennis Club, bought an ounce of coke from a dealer on the spot and doled it out to his friends. "Time to party, people," Scott said, holding aloft the little cellophane bag filled with white powder. "Party, party, party!"

101

At about this time, Margaret had a dead lock installed on the outside of Scott's door—the hallway side—just to be safe. Scott may have forgotten the morning of September 12, 1983, but she was not about to.

Chapter 22

Wayne Kerr sat in his Philadel-
phia office this gray January morning in 1985, scanning
the *Inquirer* and washing down the remains of a jelly
doughnut with another cup of the strong coffee he needed
to make it through each day. He licked the flecks of pow-
dered sugar from his sausage-thick fingers before taking
the call from Brenda Turnbull, Steven Benson's secretary
at Meridian Security. Turnbull, a whiskey-voiced brunette
whose wardrobe ran to knit dresses and low-cut, second-
skin blouses, had been assigned the task of running Margaret's personal financial statements through the Meridian
computer, so such calls had become routine. This conversation, however, was one that changed their lives forever.

❖ ❖ ❖

The neat little pile of pink slips—all notices from banks
that Meridian Marketing checks had bounced—was
growing. Meridian Marketing's office manager, Steve

103

Hawkins, picked up the phone and called Steven Benson
at Meridian Security. Again he suggested that they cut
back on expenses, reduce the overhead, and once more
Benson said no. What seemed like lavish spending to
Hawkins—a six-thousand-dollar copier when a two-thou-
sand-dollar model would do, for example—was to the customer an indication of Meridian Marketing's commitment
to quality, Steve Benson insisted. Besides, the business
would grow into these expensive toys in a few years, so
why not invest in them now? In the meantime, Benson
wanted to be sure that all bounced checks went not
through Meridian's main office in Naples, but directly to
him, to be covered out of his personal account.

Hawkins had found Steve's whole approach to running
a business anything but conventional, ever since the day
he was told that Steve Benson "of the Benson & Hedges
Bensons" wanted someone to design a sleek ad for Meridian Security, to be placed in the Naples Yellow Pages.
Benson was so pleased with Hawkins' work, he hired the
rangy, mustachioed young Floridian at a salary of thirty
thousand dollars plus expenses and gave him the high-
flown title of Vice-President, Meridian Marketing. One of
his first assignments was to design a distinctive logo for
the company, but one that no one could link with the other
Meridian firms.

◆ ◆ ◆

Brenda Turnbull, on the phone that January morning with
Wayne Kerr, wanted to know what to do about W-2 forms
for employees of Meridian Marketing. Surely she meant
Meridian Security, now really the only active company in
what Steven unselfconsciously referred to as the Meridian

"network." No, Turnbull reiterated to Kerr, she was talking about the new company, the one Steve Benson had
set up with offices in Fort Myers.

This was the first time Kerr had ever heard of an advertising and marketing company called Meridian Marketing. As soon as he was off the phone with Turnbull,
Kerr, breathing harder now, called Margaret. Dismayed,
she told her lawyer that she hadn't the slightest inkling of
what he was talking about. She had had her hands full
with Scott and his tennis career, to be sure, but if such a
company as Meridian Marketing existed, surely she would
know about it. Wouldn't she?

Kerr wasted no time booking a flight to Florida, and
within a few days he stepped off the plane in Fort Myers.
There, as storm clouds gathered for the usual afternoon
downpour, Margaret picked up Kerr in her bronze Porsche
and drove him directly to Quail Creek. Their plan of attack
was straightforward: They would confront Steven with
what they had discovered about the existence of Meridian
and demand an explanation.

The response they received was unsatisfying. Steven
shrugged, looked both Kerr and his mother square in the
eye and denied point-blank that he knew anything about
such a company, that it was as big a mystery to him as it
was to them.

In the face of such an unequivocal claim of total innocence, Kerr turned his attention to the books. If anything
fishy was going on, it would show up in the financial
records. Meridian's trailer offices on Naples' Domestic
Boulevard off Airport Road swayed as Kerr stepped in and
walked to a back room, where Steven had Brenda Turnbull
assemble the records. Kerr rolled up his sleeves and settled in for a long stint, but discovered within a matter of

minutes that the checkbook registers were a disaster. It would be pointless to even attempt to make sense of them. He gave Steven until May to get them in shape for his inspection and returned to Philadelphia.

Kerr was eager for very personal reasons to return to Philadelphia. He had a wedding to plan for—his own. On an overcast day three months later, Carol Lynn Kendall, the aspiring filmmaker, trained her lens on Kerr and his bride as they exchanged vows. A last-minute glitch of the kind that made the congenitally nervous lawyer hyperventilate had occurred: A coup in Bangkok, where Kerr's younger brother, a Marine, was security guard at the U.S. embassy, prevented his return to be best man. Another brother was in basic training and thus also unable to make it to the ceremony. Fortunately, a friend volunteered to stand up for the groom—Steve Benson.

Chapter 23

When the senior citizens center called in April of 1984 to say they had a part-time job for her, Dorothy McCormick knew what she was in for—another frantic eleventh-hour attempt by somebody to get records in order for the tax man. Margaret was indeed anxious to see her affairs put in order, but the books she handed over to McCormick were so meticulously kept—Margaret had, as always, entered every transaction in her finishing school hand—that they barely challenged the retired bookkeeper's talents. Still, Margaret was so grateful that she asked McCormick, a soft-spoken woman who sported oversized eyeglasses beneath a white pageboy hairdo, to stay on, working from 8:00 A.M. to 1:30 P.M. each day.

McCormick felt comfortable in Margaret Benson's employ, but like Joyce Quinn, she soon discovered that she had plunged into a family situation that would have made Tennessee Williams blanch. She learned not to be startled when Scott, always in a frantic rush to somewhere, suddenly appeared to demand money from Margaret.

"Why do you need it?" was Margaret's usual response. "I gave you money yesterday."

Scott would then throw his usual tantrum, and Mother would relent. These exchanges were highly civilized compared to the bouts between Scott and the visiting Carol Lynn. One morning, McCormick was working in the library of the Quail Creek house when she heard a woman's screams. The bookkeeper tentatively made her way to the hall. Carol Lynn, standing outside the open door to the bathroom, was trying to keep a towel wrapped around her with one hand as she fended off blows from Scott with the other. He kept beating her, striking her hard on the face with his open hand. Then he grabbed her by the hair and pulled her toward the living room. By now Ruby Caston, the family maid, had come running in from the kitchen. She and the bookkeeper watched in horror as Scott hit Carol Lynn again and again and yanked at her hair. The towel slipped off as he pushed her backward over a couch and, finally, onto the floor. It seemed an eternity before McCormick and the maid somehow managed to pull Scott off. Carol Lynn lay whimpering on the floor, nude.

At times like this, both Caston and McCormick wished Steven were around. Unlike the others, he never seemed to argue with Margaret about money, though once McCormick heard Steven ask his mother matter-of-factly if she gave Scott more money than she gave him. The staff had come to see Scott's big brother as the pacifier in the family, the lone peacemaker among the battling Bensons. The others sought his advice, they listened to him. Fight

with Steven? Impossible. Ask someone who knew, someone like Nancy Benson. She could have told anyone that
Steven never argued, never raised his voice. He just
walked away.

Chapter 24

Paul Harvey wished that all the Naples boat owners who hired him to skipper their yachts were more like Margaret Benson. She had no interest whatsoever in playing armchair admiral, and her instructions were to the point: When Margaret wanted to take out the *Galleon Queen*, Harvey was to have the boat gassed up and ready to go. If only dealing with her children were so simple.

This weekend morning in May, Harvey was taking the *Galleon Queen* out on a shakedown sail in preparation for a three-day cruise Margaret was planning. Steven was the first Benson to come aboard, but only for a few minutes, to check out the *Galleon Queen*'s security and surveillance system—a state-of-the-art electronic extravaganza of flashing lights and buttons designed and installed by Steven himself at a staggering cost of $250,000. The elaborate setup was utterly unnecessary for a leisure boat this size.

Steven seemed harmless enough to Harvey; Scott was another matter. Given the way the younger Benson treated family employees and others he deemed below the salt, Harvey wasted little time before pegging him as an arrogant, spoiled-rotten brat. Waving his rowdy friends aboard for the shakedown cruise, with a beer bottle in one hand and a joint in the other, Scott noisily ordered Harvey to cast off. Less than an hour later, things had got sufficiently out of hand to concern the captain. Scott had whipped out a little cellophane bag and offered its white contents to his guests, all of whom hesitated not a moment in sticking it up their noses. When Scott told Harvey to take the *Galleon Queen* on to Key West, the captain refused. Harvey was, in fact, turning the boat around and heading for home port.

"You take orders from *me*," shouted Scott, flying into one of his rages.

"I take orders from Margaret Benson," Harvey replied.

"You take orders from Bensons—that's Bensons plural," Scott shot back, "and *I am a Benson*."

Harvey was not about to risk being stopped by the coast guard with a boatful of coke fiends. He turned back over Scott's objections. But that evening, as he reported to Margaret on the day's events on the high seas, the skipper asked if Scott was right: Was Harvey to take orders from any Benson?

Margaret left no doubts on that score: "Your instructions come from one person and one person only—me."

Chapter 25

All those expensive lessons and the sixteen tennis rackets looked as if they might start to pay off in that spring of 1985, when the chance to compete on the European circuit was finally dangled in front of Scott—at twenty-one, already considered somewhat long in the tooth for a tennis newcomer. Margaret was not about to miss a golden opportunity to see Scott vindicate her. She called Carol Lynn and told her daughter that she and Scott would be flying up to Boston. Mother also wanted to squeeze in a three-day visit with an old friend, Mrs. Rothblatt, at her summer home in Lake George, New York, before hopping the plane to Oslo—the first of three stops on a circuit that was to include matches in Finland and Germany. Before leaving, Margaret sat down at her desk, opened the checkbook for the Dean Witter Reynolds account and signed two blank checks for Steven to use to meet the Meridian payroll while she and Scott were gone.

Carol Lynn was thrilled for her mother, not only because Margaret was so smitten with European travel but because, if just this once, Scott might prove to the rest of them that Margaret's faith was justified, that he had the right stuff. On arrival in Boston, however, it looked as if Scott might not get the chance. During the flight, he had begun sniffling and sneezing; by the time Scott got to Carol Lynn's Chestnut Hill house that evening, the bad case of the sniffles had turned into a full-blown head cold.

Margaret fretted about Scott's cold, but she needn't have: he kicked the virus in a couple of days, but not before passing it on to Mother. Unlike Scott's malaise, her condition worsened dramatically. She canceled the trip to Lake George in the hopes that bed rest would do the trick, but her cough persisted, and now she had a fever. On the day they were scheduled to depart for Europe from Logan Airport, Carol Lynn drove her mother to Beth Israel Hospital to be X-rayed. That afternoon, Margaret was admitted with a classic case of walking pneumonia.

There was no way they were going to keep her in the hospital. Margaret ignored doctors' warnings and instructed them to prescribe enough medication to last her through two weeks in Scandinavia and Germany. They did—with the proviso that she promise to come back to Beth Israel for a checkup as soon as she returned to the United States. Over the next week, Carol Lynn kept close tabs on Margaret; the bill from New England Telephone would show that mother and daughter had indulged in more than eight hundred dollars' worth of transatlantic chitchat.

Margaret wasn't getting any better, but that wasn't the reason Scott cut short the trip and headed home after his first loss in Norway. He had received word through his coach that he was invited to play at the U.S. Open, and didn't want to "waste any more time" in Europe when he

113

should be back in Naples, practicing. Scott hopped the first flight straight home, but Margaret kept her promise and on June 16 returned to Beth Israel for a checkup. Told that she would require chest therapy—a technique for clearing the lungs that involves turning the patient over and slapping her repeatedly on the back—Margaret balked. She had planned to return to Florida immediately and she saw no reason to alter those plans. But Carol Lynn insisted: If mother was going to be well enough to see Scott play in the U.S. Open, then she would have to stay in Boston and undergo chest therapy at the hospital every two weeks.

◆ ◆ ◆

The last thing Margaret needed was the bulletin from Wayne Kerr that Steven had secretly purchased a new house. She had been terrified for a long while that someday she might, for all her millions, somehow end up in a nursing home—that was nothing new. But Carol Lynn had never seen her quite so upset about Steven before. Scott had always been the one who scared her. God, they were both afraid of Scott—his friends, his drugs, his tantrums and violent moods. Steven, by comparison, had been a pillar of support, a dutiful son whose only major fault seemed to be too much ambition and not enough talent—business talent, anyway. After all, he didn't drink, 'gamble, take drugs, run around with rough characters. He was a family man, a devoted husband (too devoted to Debra, Margaret and Carol Lynn felt) and father of three young children.

Yet, for the first time, Margaret sensed that her son

was changing, slowly, almost imperceptibly. Steven was hard enough to read under the best of circumstances— guarded, implacable, inscrutable even when those around him flailed at one another. Margaret wondered if the notion of success and the power and money that attended it were coming to mean more to Steven than anything— maybe even more than his own family. Steven had never come to terms with his distant father; could he still be competing with his ghost?

"Steven would certainly prefer it if I weren't around," Margaret blurted out to Carol Lynn, "because it would mean more money for him if I were dead."

"Mother, that's ridiculous. What are you talking about?"

"I just wouldn't put it past Steven"—Margaret shrugged, almost matter-of-factly—"to do me in. That's all."

Carol Lynn stared back in disbelief. Mother's paranoia was clearly getting the best of her.

Margaret had always been given to hyperbole. She still caught herself smiling when she remembered Steven as a little boy, fiddling with his gadgets, trying so hard to please his father. Those memories, curiously, were more vivid now than they had ever been. And they made Steven's current behavior that much more perplexing. Hadn't she always freely given her eldest son everything he asked for? What more could she give him?

If Steven was hiding from his mother the fact that he had purchased a new house, she wanted to know why— and where the money was coming from. A half hour after Kerr called her, Margaret sat down directly opposite Carol Lynn at the kitchen table and phoned Kerr back. She

115

wanted him to get down to Naples as soon as he could clear his schedule. Together, they were going to find out what Steven was up to—once and for all.

◆ ◆ ◆

Fifteen hundred miles and worlds away from Steven, the digital bedside clock clicked to 9:30 P.M. just as Harry Hitchcock saw the crack of lightning and heard the crash that followed. The storm that was whipping through Lancaster township must have taken some unfortunate neighbor's tree with it, he thought, and toddled off to bed.

The next morning, Harry looked out the kitchen window, to see that his sixty-foot-tall oak tree had smashed to earth not fifteen feet from the house, uprooting hundreds of his prize tulips and azaleas. As omens went, they did not get much more powerful.

Chapter 26

It was off-season in Florida, so the hordes of T-shirted tourists and white-crested snow-birds in flamingo-pink bermudas who would normally cram K mart on a holiday weekend were mercifully absent. Carol Lynn, in her ever-present floppy white hat and self-conscious Greta Garbo shades, moved effortlessly from aisle to aisle in search of all the odds and ends she would be needing to help stake out Mother's new building lots. (Amid all the turmoil, Margaret had somehow managed to buy three adjoining Quail Creek parcels on which to erect her permanent dwelling—a spectacular 28,000-square-foot villa to outshine every other Quail Creek mansion.) As always, Carol Lynn knew precisely what her job would require: wooden stakes (color-coded dowels, actually), cans of paint, some string. Steven already had one of those big measuring wheels that roll along the ground—the kind police use to measure off a crime scene—and she knew there was a tape measure somewhere around the house. She loaded everything into the Porsche, satisfied that she had all the materials she needed to make precise measurements. Carol Lynn, unlike Steven and Scott, tended to do things very precisely.

A few miles away, not far from the Meridian Security trailer, Jeff Maynes just happened to glance at his watch— it was not quite three twenty-five when a man who said he worked for the Del Rey Construction Company walked into Hughes Supply and asked to buy two four-inch-wide pipe end caps. While the customer filled out the invoice, Maynes fetched the pipe from the back, then stuffed the caps in a brown paper bag with the pink customer's copy of the invoice. Maynes glanced down at the invoice and tried to read the signature, but it was totally illegible, a left-handed hieroglyphic. This wasn't the first construction worker he'd seen with lousy penmanship. He looked up, to deliver his usual "Have a nice day," but no one was there. Maynes shrugged and printed "Del Rey Construction" on the invoice. Then he filed it away and took his break.

❖ ❖ ❖

It struck Carol Lynn as more than a little unusual when her brother showed up at Quail Creek that Saturday afternoon to tag along, even though he explained he was in the neighborhood anyway to fix a Meridian-installed burglar alarm that had malfunctioned up the street. But she and Mother needed the help, and they weren't about to question his motives now. Nothing was said about Meridian Marketing or the house or the missing checks as the three of them piled into the four-wheel-drive Suburban, with Steven behind the wheel. Carol Lynn sat in the bucket seat on the right front passenger side, and Mother

The victims. Shortly before she left for a new life in Florida, Margaret Benson struck a hopeful pose at her Lancaster home. Only after the murders was it revealed that Scott was not Margaret's son but her grandson; Scott's real mother was Margaret's daughter Carol Lynn.
AP/WIDE WORLD PHOTOS

Wayne Kerr, Margaret Benson's lawyer and confidant, was inside the Benson house at the time of the blast. He would be a key witness against Steven Benson.
LAURA ELLIOTT/FORT MYERS NEWS-PRESS

An aerial shot of 13002 White Violet Drive taken shortly after the bomb blasts that killed Margaret and Scott. A plastic sheet covers the wreckage.
ERIC STRACHAN/NAPLES DAILY NEWS

Sole survivor Carol Lynn Benson Kendall is wheeled to an ambulance in critical condition.
AP/WIDE WORLD PHOTOS

The two strategically placed pipe bombs left the Bensons' Chevrolet Suburban a tangle of charred, twisted metal.
AP/WIDE WORLD PHOTOS

Graveside at the funeral of Margaret and Scott. White-maned Harry Hitchcock sat in stunned silence, flanked by Margaret's sister Janet Lee and grandson Steven Benson (left) and wife Debbie. *Right:* Steven and Debbie holding hands leaving the funeral.

AP/WIDE WORLD PHOTOS

State Attorney Joe D'Alessandro announcing the arrest of Steven Benson for the murders of Margaret and Scott Benson.
ERIC STRACHAN/NAPLES DAILY NEWS

Carol Lynn Benson Kendall, her head still bandaged, arrives in Florida to provide the emotional testimony that will lead to her brother's indictment for murder.
ERIC STRACHAN/NAPLES DAILY NEWS

Texas attorney Margaret Covington (left) helped the defense team in picking jury members (below). Covington herself faced charges in Texas of hiring two men to assault the father of her out-of-wedlock child.
GARTH FRANCIS/FORT MYERS NEWS-PRESS
LAURA ELLIOTT/FORT MYERS NEWS-PRESS

Defense attorneys Jerry Berry (left) and Michael McDonnell back up their client during the prosecution's opening arguments. AP/WIDE WORLD PHOTOS

Judge Hugh Hayes
ERIC STRACHAN/NAPLES DAILY
NEWS

For the prosecution:
Dwight and Jerry, the
Battling Brothers Brock.
ERIC STRACHAN/NAPLES DAILY
NEWS

Her face still terribly scarred, onetime beauty queen Carol Lynn arrives to testify against her brother.
MARC BEAUDIN/FORT MYERS NEWS-PRESS

Dwight Brock wheels the prosecution's papers into the courtroom in a shopping cart.
ERIC STRACHAN/NAPLES DAILY NEWS

Clasping his hand on Steven Benson's shoulder, McDonnell makes his emotional opening statement.
ERIC STRACHAN/NAPLES DAILY NEWS

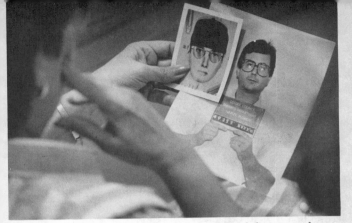

One juror compares a police artist's sketch of the man who bought pipe at Hughes Supply to a mug shot of Steven Benson. TOM PRICE/FORT MYERS NEWS-PRESS

Michael McDonnell's mother-in-law, Mafalda Gray, had so many friendly chats with Steven Benson that reporters dubbed her "Rent-a-Mom." AP/WIDE WORLD PHOTOS

Chuck Meyer, who pulled
Carol Lynn from the fiery
Suburban, tells the jury how
far away he was when the
second bomb went off.
LAURA ELLIOTT/FORT MYERS
NEWS-PRESS

Lieutenant Harold Young
was surprised at how calm
Steven Benson appeared
the morning of the
killings.
ERIC STRACHAN/NAPLES DAILY
NEWS

Scott Benson's psychiatrist,
Dr. José Lombillo, testified for
the defense. He told jurors
that Scott was violence-prone
and addicted to laughing gas.
ERIC STRACHAN/NAPLES DAILY
NEWS

Paul Harvey, captain of
Margaret's yacht, refused
to take Scott and his coke-
snorting friends to Key West
aboard the *Galleon Queen*.
ERIC STRACHAN/NAPLES DAILY
NEWS

On the stand for six hours, ATF auditor Diana Galloway used charts to trace the flow of funds from Margaret's accounts through Meridian into Steven's pocket.
LAURA ELLIOTT/FORT MYERS NEWS-PRESS

At Hughes Supply, ATF investigator Terry Hopkins uncovered two invoices for pipe; the invoices bore Steven Benson's palm prints.
LAURA ELLIOTT/FORT MYERS NEWS-PRESS

Jurors gasped when explosives expert Al Gleason, under questioning by Jerry Brock, produced a facsimile of the 27-pound pipe bombs used to kill Margaret and Scott.
LAURA ELLIOTT/FORT MYERS NEWS-PRESS

Using an aerial photo, Carol Lynn describes for Jerry Brock and the jury the scene the morning of the bombings.
LAURA ELLIOTT/FORT MYERS NEWS-PRESS

Scott's girlfriend, Kim Beegle, delivered some of the trial's most emotional testimony.
ERIC STRACHAN/NAPLES DAILY NEWS

Steven weeps as Michael McDonnell describes him as a "loving son."
LAURA ELLIOTT/FORT MYERS NEWS-PRESS

Family patriarch Harry Hitchcock, 89, arrived in court at the end of the trial to "lend moral support" to Carol Lynn.

TOM PRICE/FORT MYERS NEWS-PRESS

Steven's secretary, Brenda Turnbull, testified on behalf of her boss, but broke down under cross-examination.
TOM PRICE/FORT MYERS NEWS-PRESS

Voices from the grave: Steven sobbed again as defense lawyer Jerry Berry played a tape recording of Scott and Margaret arguing bitterly.
ERIC STRACHAN/NAPLES DAILY NEWS

During closing arguments, Mike McDonnell disputes palm print evidence linking his client to the murders.
ERIC STRACHAN/NAPLES DAILY NEWS

Prosecutor Jerry Brock asks the jury to impose the death penalty.
ERIC STRACHAN/NAPLES DAILY NEWS

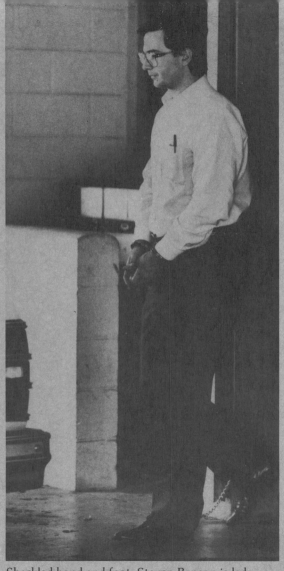

Shackled hand and foot, Steven Benson is led away to begin serving consecutive life sentences.
AP/WIDE WORLD PHOTOS

took her usual place in the back seat, behind her daughter.
This arrangement made sense from everyone's perspective: Mother hated the air conditioning that blasted in the front, Carol Lynn sometimes got carsick if she sat in the back and, raised consciousness of the 1980s notwithstanding, it had always seemed logical for the eldest son to drive.

It hardly mattered. No sooner did they get out of the Suburban at the site than a cloud of mosquitoes enveloped them. They had no choice but to pile back into the Suburban and return home; Margaret had forgotten to bring the repellent. When they got home, Carol Lynn left the stakes in the Suburban but insisted on bringing the cans of paint into the house. She was afraid that, in this oppressive heat, they might explode.

That evening, Margaret continued to fume about Steven's secret purchase of a new house. As Margaret vented her fears and frustrations, Carol Lynn could not remember her mother ever being this upset before—not even when she learned that Carol Lynn was pregnant with Scott, or that Tracy Mullins was pregnant by him. After dinner, Carol Lynn joined her mother in the living room to watch Margaret's favorite television show: *Murder, She Wrote*.

Chapter 27

The lapels of his suit wilted in Florida's stultifying summer sun as Kerr stepped off an Eastern Airlines jetliner in Fort Myers that Sunday, July 7, at twelve-thirty and walked briskly toward Margaret's waiting Porsche. They made their way south to Naples on Route 41. The pavement ahead shimmered in the heat.

That evening at Quail Creek, they mapped out their strategy as Carol Lynn looked over plot plans for the new house. First, they would see for themselves whether a company called Meridian Marketing really existed, and just what kind of house Steven was now living in. Then there was the matter of the two checks she had signed before going to Europe—where were they, what had they been used for, and for how much?

The next morning, they sped straight to the Meridian Security trailer, where Brenda Turnbull and the rest of the staff had been told by Steven that his mother was being audited and Kerr was coming down to help her with her taxes. When the two of them arrived, however, Steven was nowhere in evidence. Now that she was back in the country, Margaret said to Turnbull, without a trace of anger or upset in her voice, she and Kerr were eager to see Steven's new house in Fort Myers and the Meridian Marketing offices. Armed with the addresses for both, Margaret and Kerr zoomed north, back to Fort Myers and a place called Brynwood.

On his return to the Meridian Security trailer, Steven asked Brenda where his mother and Kerr had disappeared to, and was puzzled by the secretary's evasive answer. He didn't press her; instead he picked up the phone to call the one person who would be certain to know their whereabouts.

Back at Quail Creek, Carol Lynn hunched over the dining room table, chewing on a pencil as she pored over the architect's drawings. She had come down with Mother to watch over her recovery and help with plans for the new house. It was going to look out over one of Quail Creek's man-made lakes, and Margaret, who seemed to prize view above all else in a house, had been careful to choose property on a lake that Quail Creek's developers planned to enlarge even further. Carol Lynn worried that her mother's architects might not be, well, creative enough in their approach, so she took it upon herself to make sure that every window was canted in precisely the right way to soak up those spectacular lake views.

She had been struggling with the architect's drawings for hours when her work was interrupted by the call from Steven. "Mother there?" he asked. Carol Lynn could easily detect the poorly disguised tension in her brother's voice.

"No."

"How about Wayne?"

121

"No." She was beginning to like playing dumb.

"Do you know where they went?"

"Uh-uh."

"Do you know when they'll be back?"

"No, I don't. Why do you need Mother and Wayne?" she asked.

"Well, I have some appointments and I'll be out of the office in case they want to see me."

"Why don't you just leave a list of places where you'll be?" Carol Lynn was really enjoying this; Steven had always been the one who would disappear in the middle of a workday, not bothering to tell anybody what he was doing or where he was going.

"No, I'll call back." As he hung up, Steven got Steve Hawkins on the line and warned him that his mother and Wayne Kerr were on the way. At all costs, he was to take the office computer—the computer that contained all the Meridian Marketing records—and hide it. Hawkins was already miffed at all the cloak-and-dagger maneuvers, but he dutifully unplugged the terminal and carried it, along with the printer, out to the trunk of his car well before the unwelcome visitors arrived at Meridian Marketing. When they did, Margaret and Wayne Kerr said nothing to Hawkins. They did not even get out of the car. No need. They had seen enough to prove that Steven had been lying about the existence of a sixth Meridian company all along.

The next stop was Brynwood, a pine-shaded enclave of forty-seven homes on the southern perimeter of Fort Myers. Margaret was not prepared for what she saw when she pulled up to Brynwood's electronically controlled iron security gates. Kerr said nothing as they sat in front of No. 7, a shake-roofed estate complete with tennis courts, Olympic-sized pool and cabana. Steven's blue Datsun

280Z was parked outside, just opposite the tennis courts. One of Meridian Security's own blue panel trucks, with the red and black logo, was also there; Margaret guessed correctly that Steven was seeing to it that his house had the best security money could buy.

Kerr had never seen his boss so livid. They sat in the car, staring at the house, for several minutes before she spoke. "How could he do this?" Her voice was tinged with despair. Certainly the knowledge that Debra had taken up residence in this palace only made matters worse. "My own son, taking my money, *lying to me.*" Kerr nodded. "I don't know what to do anymore. I really have grave doubts about Steven as a son." Maybe she should disinherit Steven once and for all, she said in disgust.

"Well, maybe the better route to take," Kerr suggested calmly, "would be to get an accounting for these loans and treat them as advances against Steven's share of the estate."

There was a long silence before Margaret spoke. "I want to know what I can do to get it back, Wayne. I want to put a lien on this house and that car and everything he owns if that's what it takes to get my money back."

They would not confront Steven, but rather draw in the net slowly, subtly. Get the goods on him first. Let him hang himself. It was two-thirty when Margaret and Kerr arrived back at the Meridian trailer in Naples. Brenda was at her desk, smoking a cigarette and reading a book. They walked to Steven's office at the other end of the trailer and shut the door behind them. Brenda, having sat through Carol Lynn's unselfconscious battles with Margaret over things like chandeliers and bathroom tile, braced herself. But instead of a knock-down-drag-out, there was only the muffled sound of businesslike conversation coming from

123

Steven's office. Ever so gently, Margaret mentioned that she had heard about her son's new house. Steven didn't miss a beat. He merely explained that he had sold the Datsun to make the down payment. They didn't tell him that they had seen the car parked square in front of his new house.

Once again, Steven left Kerr alone with the records. Margaret, in a separate office, busied herself getting together the welter of Dean Witter Reynolds statements. The balance on the Active Assets Account alone now hovered around the six-million-dollar mark.

Steven had to get out. It was, as always this time of year, stifling outside, and though Steven never wore a hat, he asked around to see if anyone had a baseball cap he might borrow. No one seemed to have one.

Kerr shook his head in dismay. The checkbook registers were in no better shape than the last time he had tried to make sense of them, back in January. Kerr went to Steven's office to tell him they'd be digging in for a long night's work with the books, but Steven was nowhere to be found.

◆ ◆ ◆

Like most Monday afternoons near quitting time, Hughes Supply was not jammed to the rafters with patrons, so when the bearlike man wearing small, round shades and a dark-blue baseball cap lumbered into the store, James Link filled his order instantly—two galvanized metal pipes, each measuring one foot in length and four inches in diameter.

Link, a bespectacled, gray-haired man in his late fifties, courted a hernia when he lugged the two heavy pipes out

124

and dropped them on the counter. The customer pulled a couple of neatly folded twenties from his pants pocket and, after scrawling his name on the invoice, picked up his merchandise easily and turned to leave. Now Link remembered where he'd seen sunglasses like that—on John Lennon. They were the same wire-rimmed, perfectly spherical and totally opaque glasses that the Beatle had liked to wear.

◆ ◆ ◆

Perhaps an hour had passed before Steven once again materialized in his office. Margaret was not pleased with the state of the books. "Look," she said, "we'll all stay here and work on this together all night if we have to, but we've got to get the books straightened out for the IRS."

Steven declined. He had a social engagement, he explained, one that he couldn't break this late in the game. In fact, Steven went on, he intended to knock off work early.

Margaret tried to mask her rage. She was not about to let him get away this time. Scooping the records off the desk, she shoved them into Steven's arms. "In that case," said Margaret, "take these home with you and have them ready by tomorrow."

◆ ◆ ◆

Carol Lynn, still laboring over the architect's drawings, was surprised to hear from Steven twice in the same day. He told her that he was going to come over to the house the next morning to help stake out Margaret's new property. "And we'll take Scott along," he added.

Why in the world, she thought to herself, would he ever in a million years ask Scott to come along? It was one thing for Steven to suddenly make an unsolicited offer of help, but to include Scott? At worst, the youngest member of the family could be a spoiled, miserable little SOB. At best, well, not exactly the sort to lend a helping hand.

"I'll be over early," Steven went on.

"What do you mean by 'early'?" Carol Lynn asked. Steven was not known for getting up with the chickens.

"How about seven-thirty?"

"Okay." Restrain yourself, Carol Lynn thought. Don't ask any questions. Help is help.

◆ ◆ ◆

When her mother walked in the front door that afternoon with Kerr, Carol Lynn wasted no time in telling her about the conversation. "You'll never guess who called to volunteer to help us stake out the lot. Steven *offered* to drive us over there."

"Steven? *Our* Steven?" blurted Margaret in not-quite-mock amazement. Then she pulled out the Yellow Pages and began searching for the name of a restaurant. It was July 8—Carol Lynn's forty-first birthday—and as much as she might have wanted to forget the accelerating passage of time, Carol Lynn assented when her Mother invited her out for a celebration dinner. Everybody was exhausted from the day's events, so what they were in the market for was a place that not only was close to Quail Creek and open on a Monday, but that also served dinner early. They settled on The Plum, a suburban-chic restaurant just minutes away, across from the Pavilion Shopping Center on Route 41.

The birthday girl was not center stage during dinner. Quite the contrary. Steven was Topic A. There were many things regarding her son Margaret had let slide by, but the house in Brynwood would not be one of them. This was, as Margaret was fond of saying, the straw that broke the camel's back. She talked with Kerr about how they would track down those two checks she had presigned before she left for Europe. Those missing checks, Margaret suspected, were the key. If they yielded the evidence she thought they would, proving embezzlement, she would have no choice but to follow Kerr's advice: either pull out of Meridian altogether, or fire Steven as president.

After dinner, Mother phoned Paul Harvey, captain of the *Galleon Queen*, and told him to get the yacht ready for a cruise. He was to call Margaret back the next day for more detailed instructions. Then she returned to her strategy session with Kerr. Listening to Wayne and Mother spin their web around Steven, Carol Lynn could not help but feel as if she were watching a spy movie. It was almost a letdown to go home that night and watch *Scarecrow and Mrs. King*. After sitting through an hour that couldn't compare with the intrigue right under their roof, Carol Lynn excused herself when a program she detested, *Kate & Allie*, came on the air. *Kate & Allie* was another of Mother's favorites. It was not quite nine-twenty when Carol Lynn pulled down the sheets and climbed into bed. The musical sound of Mother's laughter carried down the hall.

◆ ◆ ◆

Steve Hawkins had been there a little more than four hours, much of it spent sitting in the living room in Steven Benson's nearly empty new house, when he checked the

127

time. It was 11:00 P.M. and Hawkins had to admit he'd had an enjoyable evening—though he would have preferred a bit more notice. Being called by the boss at 6:00 P.M. and summoned for dinner at seven struck Steve Hawkins as more than a little inconsiderate. Still, Hawkins felt he had better oblige. Steve Benson was the president of Meridian Marketing, and if Debra was going to the trouble of preparing dinner, the company's vice-president had better be there.

Most of the evening, as it turned out, was devoted to chatting about business, and when it was over, the host showed as much consideration for his guest as he had when he'd invited him. He came into the living room in his pajamas, bid Hawkins good night and disappeared down the hall to the bedroom.

Chapter 28

For more than an hour, Scott's dog, Buck, waited patiently in the parked Suburban, a sweltering hotbox in this ninety-eight-degree heat, while Kim and Scott test-drove a Camaro he had said he'd buy her. After they left the Chevy dealership, Buck found himself waiting in another parking lot. This time, the killer attack dog panted and slobbered and waved his tail cheerfully for two hours as T-shirted shoppers padded past on their way to and from Fort Myers' sprawling Edison Mall. One reached the mall from the center of town by driving a few miles south on 41, past the Dairy Queens, Burger Kings and Taco Bells that in this part of the country are only slightly less abundant than pelicans and palmetto bugs. Just a few blocks away is Thomas Edison's winter estate, a slice of Victorian gingerbread that, second only to the white-sand shelling beaches of nearby Sanibel and Captiva islands, ranks among the vicinity's top tourist attractions. It is doubtful that more than a tiny fraction of the thousands of shoppers who stream into the Edison

Mall each day have ever bothered to make the short side trip to the 101-year-old Edison house. Nevertheless, those bound for Sears, The Gap and Radio Shack must first pass by a huge beige-and-brown stucco bas-relief of the scowling inventor at the mall's main entrance.

Buck barked a greeting to his owners as they approached the Suburban laden with packages. After a marathon three-hour search, Kim, holding Scott to his original promise of one new outfit a week, had picked up some clothes at a boutique that catered to women of her petite size. They were moving almost before Kim had the chance to slam her door shut; frenetic Scott, as was his custom, had left the keys in the ignition for an expeditious getaway.

From the mall, they headed for dinner at a popular seafood restaurant called The Shallows, but first they stopped at a gas station so that Kim could change into the jumpsuit she had just purchased.

She had a little something extra for Scott—pot, the only nasty habit he was not willing to give up even for his once-in-a-lifetime shot at the U.S. Open and the big time. Although she had not used it for about a year, Kim dutifully rolled him a joint, and when he was finished, put the roach in a Baggie that was already partially filled with the stringy brown residue of their half-smoked joints.

At The Shallows, Scott abstained from alcohol. Kim ordered an expensive bottle of wine, then sent it back. Next, they bar-hopped from The Mason Jar to The Brassy, then on to a pizza joint. Scott sipped ginger ale, Kim Michelob Lite.

The house in Quail Creek was dark when Scott and Kim pulled up a little before midnight. Kim fetched her purse from the console between them, then grabbed the bags out of the back seat.

The couple used the private entrance to Scott's room. While Kim took off her makeup in the bathroom and got ready for bed, Scott sneaked the dog inside. Buck promptly dozed off next to the door while the lovers lay in bed, giggling and fantasizing about a life away from Margaret, about marriage, even the details of their wedding ceremony. On one thing they were in complete agreement: they both wanted a Key Lime wedding cake.

Chapter 29

For whatever reason, Margaret had never gotten around to hanging drapes in the guest quarters. So Wayne Kerr was indeed rudely awakened when six forty-five rolled around and the yellow-white Florida morning sun flooded the room. Kerr knew Steve was expected around seven-thirty—Carol Lynn and Margaret had made such an issue of the early hour—and wanted to beat him into the kitchen at all costs. Steve was one of the few of his client "friends" whose appetite was nearly as voracious as Kerr's. Still, it took twenty minutes for Kerr to summon the energy to get out of bed and stagger into the bathroom.

Too late. Kerr hurriedly stepped out of the shower, toweled himself off and was rushing to put on his clothes when, from the guest room window, he could see Steve's beige Chevy van pulling up to the front of the house.

Margaret and Carol Lynn had been up chatting for an hour in the kitchen when they heard the crunching sound of gravel as the van pulled into the drive. In his room, Kerr straightened his tie—since the plan was to have Margaret drop him off at Meridian Security to go over the books after she staked out the lot, he thought it best to wear a suit—tucked some paperwork under his pudgy arm and straggled into the kitchen. It had been some time since he glimpsed the van, but Steve was still nowhere to be seen.

A few more moments passed before Margaret asked her daughter to find out if indeed it was Steven. Walking to the back door leading to the garage, Carol Lynn could see that the van had been parked at an acute angle to the Suburban; she could look directly through the van's windshield and see Steven bent over at the rear of both vehicles. His head was down, his shoulders moving. As if he were lifting something, she thought. "What is he doing out there?" Carol Lynn mumbled to herself impatiently, though she really couldn't have cared less at the time. She wouldn't get a straight answer anyway, so why even bother asking. She went back into the kitchen. "Steven's here," she announced.

He waltzed through the front door. "Good morning, Steven," said Margaret half-mockingly.

Steven nodded. "Scott up?"

While Margaret went to roust Scott out of bed, Steven turned to Carol Lynn, who by now had abandoned the architect's plans altogether and was stationed at the living room coffee table, painstakingly working on her own design for the new house. Steven asked Carol Lynn where she had stashed the supplies for today's expedition.

"Everything's all together underneath the counter in the kitchen," she said, pointing to the built-in Formica cabinet. "I had Kim and Scott clear all their junk out of the drawers so I'd have room for everything there." Steven headed for the kitchen, picked up the stakes, string

133

and paint, and carried them out the front door just as Scott stumbled in, wearing only a pair of shorts and wiping the sleep from his eyes.

"Why do you have to get me up?"

"Steven wants you to help us stake out the lot," Margaret explained.

Scott grumbled, but went back into his room to get dressed.

Kerr was heating up a pot of water and getting ready to make some Sanka—Margaret kept only decaffeinated coffee around—when Steven, now oddly ebullient, walked back into the kitchen. "Oh, Wayne," he said, "you don't want to drink that instant stuff. I'm going to drive over to the Shop & Go and get some real coffee. As a matter of fact, since you're on a diet, I'll get you some Danish too. Anybody else want something? Doughnuts?"

Carol Lynn was nonplussed. "Why," she asked, "didn't you get the coffee on the way in?" Steve ignored her. "Mother?" When Margaret shook her head that she wasn't interested, Steve headed for the door.

Mother and Carol Lynn shook their heads, and Steve bounced out the door. The van was low on gas, and even though the Shop & Go was just five minutes away, Steven said he thought it best to be safe and take the Suburban. The keys were, as always, in the ignition, where Scott had left them.

Nearly an hour passed, and by now Marty Taylor—a neatly turned out widow who augmented her income as Margaret's personal secretary by moonlighting as a part-time manicurist—had arrived in her white Chevette. She and Kerr sat diagonally across from one another at the rattan table in the lanai, trying to untangle Margaret's accounts.

The round trip to the Shop & Go shouldn't have taken more than fifteen or twenty minutes. Still dressed in her robe, Carol Lynn said, "I wonder what on earth happened to him?"

"At this rate"—Kerr looked at his watch—"he could have driven all the way back to Fort Myers to get the coffee." Carol Lynn was starting to worry that her brother may have been in an accident, when finally he came in the door. It was nearly eight-forty.

Kerr and Steve popped the lids off the Styrofoam cups and chugalugged their coffees. Within minutes, the only evidence that Steven had ever picked up doughnuts and pastries were the crumbs that speckled Margaret's kitchen counter. They were ready to head out the door, when Marty Taylor remembered: at nine, a swimming pool salesman was supposed to stop by to take some measurements and give them an estimate on what it would cost to build a pool behind the house. Margaret thought adding a pool would boost the price when it was time to sell this house and move into the new one.

"Oh, that's right," said Margaret. "Somebody's got to be here for the pool people."

Steven looked worried. "Mother, you'll have to come along. I really want you to."

"What do I have to come along for?" There was more than a little irritation in Margaret's tone.

"Well, there are things I want you to see. . . . Besides," Steven added, "Wayne will be here and he can get a price from the pool people."

Mother did not see how Kerr was going to be able to stand in for her, and Kerr agreed. "I'm the least construction-minded of the whole group," he protested.

"Sure, it's easy," Steven reassured him, then drew a

135

diagram on a yellow legal pad, giving dimensions, where he wanted the lights, the tile, the steps. "Here," he said, handing the drawing to Kerr. "Just tell them we'll pay the price for something like this, measuring fifteen by thirty."

"Steven, it's not going to work," Carol Lynn objected. "It's ridiculous. Mother should be here to tell them what kind of pool she wants. If she isn't, it'll be like getting a quote on apples when you wanted to buy oranges."

Scott, seemingly oblivious of all the quarreling, sauntered into the room in sandals. The phone was ringing and he picked it up. He told his coach he would be late for practice. Finally, after a solid ten minutes of bickering, Steven came up with a solution: "Look, Mother, when the pool man gets here, Marty will drive over to the lot to get you and bring you back." Marty didn't mind. The lot was only five minutes away.

Mother changed out of her high heels into some tennis shoes, while Carol Lynn scooped the blueprints off the living room table and began her customary search for her shoes and the dark glasses she misplaced at least a half dozen times a day (she was allergic to the fabric covering Margaret's furniture, which made her eyes even more sensitive than they normally were). Carol Lynn poured a Coke into an ice-filled insulated plastic glass and finally headed out the door.

Steven helped his mother up into the passenger seat of the trucklike Suburban and she buckled up while Scott slid behind the wheel. When Carol Lynn came out of the house, the whole seating arrangement struck her as strange—Scott in the driver's seat instead of Steven, Margaret in the front seat where Carol Lynn usually sat to avoid getting carsick in the back, and Steven perched half in, half out the right rear side, the door open. The notion of saying something flitted across her mind, but Carol Lynn decided for once not to make a fuss—it was a short trip, after all.

"Who's got the keys?" Margaret asked impatiently. It was Sahara-hot, and the air conditioning in the Suburban had not been working.

"I've got the keys," answered Steven.

"Then give them to Scott." As Steven walked around the back of the car to Scott, he put his hand on his sister's derriere and gave her a little boost up into the cab. How nice, Carol Lynn thought. Steven really wasn't in the habit of helping his sister. He reached through the open window and handed the keys to Scott. They dangled on the end of a paper clip.

Steven turned to get back into the Suburban when he began checking his pockets for something. "Darn," he said, shaking his head. "I forgot the tape measure." With that, he walked around the front of the Suburban toward the house. Carol Lynn left her door propped open to let what little air there was circulate. Meantime, she was busy trying to balance the huge roll of blueprints and the Coke; she knew there'd be hell to pay from Mother if she spilled her drink all over the upholstery. Carol Lynn had placed the glass precariously on the seat as she got in; now she bent over to retrieve it. When she looked back up, she saw only Mother and Scott sitting there. Steven had vanished from sight. Scott leaned over and extended his right arm. Carol Lynn thought he was trying to switch on the air conditioning. He was turning the ignition key. There was the sound of a click. . . .

It was nine-eighteen.

PART THREE

THE
MURDERS

"Anyone capable of murdering
his mother for money is capable
of murdering his grandfather
for the same reason."
—HARRY HITCHCOCK

Chapter 30

"Oh, my God!" said Kerr. "What was that?" Marty Taylor stared across the ledgers and computer printouts in disbelief. Houses as far as a quarter mile away shook. ("I thought it was another construction accident," someone would later say. "Not someone murdering my neighbor.") At first, Kerr thought the Lotus might have backfired—he knew they'd been having trouble with it—until what sounded like pebbles started pelting the windows of the lanai. At this point, the phone rang and Marty Taylor answered it, while Kerr went to check out the commotion in front of the house. On the other end of the line, Paul Harvey was calling to talk to Margaret about her plans for a cruise aboard the *Galleon Queen*.

Kerr made it halfway from the lanai to the front door when Steven came bursting in. "Call an ambulance!" Steven ordered. Harvey was on hold. "There's been an explosion," Marty told him. "The family was in the truck. Why don't you call back Friday?" She hung up.

Kerr picked up the phone just as another blast rocked the house; his mind suddenly went blank. What was the emergency number? Marty told him to dial 911, and Kerr, stunned, managed to do it. He blurted out that there had been an explosion. Steven stood next to him, his hands trembling violently. He searched his pockets for a cigarette. "Do you need a fire engine?" the voice on the other end asked. Kerr froze. Marty grabbed the phone and told them to send a fire engine.

Now safe on the lawn across the street, Carol Lynn watched Steven burst out of the front door and begin running around the burning Suburban, tearing at his hair. He was screaming hysterically. From her vantage point, it looked almost as if Steven was running directly into the fire. Carol Lynn was reminded of keening mourners in Beirut, throwing themselves on the coffins of their loved ones.

Within minutes, 13002 White Violet Drive was teaming with strangers—golfers, the crew of the garbage truck, construction workers from down the street, firemen, police. Chuck Meyer, who moments before had pulled Carol Lynn to safety, just as the second blast occurred, stood nearby, holding a handkerchief to what remained of his nose. The puncture in Meyer's chest from the shrapnel was making a saucer-sized bloodstain on his Lacoste shirt. Still in shock when the paramedics arrived, Carol Lynn seemed unaware of the extent to which she had been burned. Instead, she was angry that the female paramedic who was first on the scene didn't try to revive Scott. She could see him lying there, alone. He had barely a scratch on him. Barely a scratch . . .

While the paramedics strapped Carol Lynn onto a stretcher for the trip to Naples Community Hospital, Paul

Hardy, the son of Quail Creek's developer, went to see what he could do for Steven. He had calmed down now, and asked Hardy if he could fetch some cigarettes from the front seat of the beige van, the van Steven had driven there that morning, loaded with all the financial records Margaret and Kerr had asked to see. The van was parked dangerously close to the flaming Suburban. "We'd better get it out of there," said Meyer's golf partner, Ralph Merrill, "before it blows." Hardy hopped behind the wheel of the van and reached to turn on the ignition, when it struck him that this was not the most prudent thing in the world to do. Who knew how many bombs had been planted, or where? He took the cigarettes off the seat and brought them back to Steven. Not long after, a member of the bomb squad gingerly disengaged the ignition and scoured the van for any other unpleasant surprises. When he reconnected the ignition, he noticed that the tank was about one quarter full.

Collier County sheriff's deputies swarmed over the block like carpenter ants, talking to witnesses, marking off the scene with police tape, checking beneath the yellow sheets that covered the bodies, waving away the curious. Within hours, they were joined by special agents from the federal Bureau of Alcohol, Tobacco and Firearms, who had been ordered to comb the area for "anything that didn't grow." Wearing magnetic gloves, several ATF agents squatted in the driveway, methodically sifting the soil beneath and around the Suburban for whatever fragments of evidence might remain. Others found pieces of fabric, metal and flesh in the trees, even on the roof. Neighbors would later hire a special cleaning service to remove bits of flesh that had been blown onto their screens.

Inside the house, pandemonium quickly gave way to

143

an oddly relaxed atmosphere. Kerr, though clearly shaken, had stopped hyperventilating. Marty sat silent while Steve, a smoldering cigarette in his hand, talked with Lieutenant Harold Young from the Collier County Sheriff's Department. For the first time, he explained why it had taken him more than an hour to drive to the Shop & Go. Steven was going in to buy coffee when he ran into two workers from the Sandcastle Construction Company. He didn't know their names, and no matter how many times Young would press him on this today, Steve evaded the question of just who those construction workers were.

Young couldn't complain. Steve Benson was being extremely cooperative and good-natured for a man whose mother and brother were lying murdered in the front yard and who himself had miraculously escaped death. He had, Steven told Lieutenant Young, walked just three steps—maybe nine feet at the most—when the Suburban blew. He accommodatingly agreed to change out of his short-sleeved shirt and his jeans so that they could be analyzed for any debris, and seemed only mildly perturbed when the police said they were too busy to dispatch a car to Fort Myers to pick up his wife. He called Meridian Security and asked Steve Hawkins to do it.

On the ride up, Debbie seemed less concerned about what had happened than with what was supposed to have happened. Someone, she kept saying, was out to kill Steven. Scott and Margaret just happened to be at the wrong place at the wrong time. But Steven was alive, and there was still someone lurking out there who did not want him to be. When they arrived at the house later that morning, Hawkins, grim-faced, walked up to his boss to offer his condolences. But before Hawkins could say anything,

Benson spoke. "Well," he asked, "how much money did
we make today?"

In the driveway of a house two doors away, the glint of metal caught the eye of portly, mustachioed sheriff's deputy Roy Williams. A veteran of twelve years on the force, he knew enough not to touch the small shard of galvanized pipe. The crime technicians first had to photograph it right where it was, then would carefully place it in a plastic bag, for tests and analyses of all sorts back at the lab.

The bomb squad moved into the house and began searching to make sure that whoever planted the bomb in the Suburban hadn't left a calling card indoors. Debra came out of a back bathroom and asked what was going on. When they told her, she shook her head in disbelief. "You mean there I was, sitting on the pot," she said, "and I could have been *blown up?*" Everyone laughed.

In Margaret's bedroom closet, the police found two brightly wrapped packages. They were presents for the previous December birthdays of her grandchildren Christopher and Victoria—presents that Margaret was never allowed to deliver.

Chapter 31

"Okay, Carol," said the man in the surgeon's mask standing at her hospital bedside. "I'm a detective from the sheriff's office."

"Oh, where are you?"

"I'm over here on your left-hand side."

It was 4:30 P.M.—a little over seven hours after the explosion—and Carol Lynn was listed in critical condition. She was coherent though somewhat groggy now, but given the extent of her burns, there was no telling if she was going to make it. Since she was the sole survivor of the blast, it seemed unlikely that there could be a more important witness in the case. Carol Lynn's doctors would allow the police to talk to her, but for no more than fifteen minutes at a time, after which she would require at least one full hour of sleep.

After she was reassured that she did not have to have her attorney present while she answered a few questions, Carol Lynn proceeded, her speech only slightly slurred by the painkillers that flowed through the IV, to provide a

chillingly dispassionate account of the crime. To the investigators' amazement, only once did she become emotional—her voice breaking when she described the explosion itself and the sensation that she was being
electrocuted, pulled down an orange tunnel by some malevolent force.

Not long after the interview was over, Carol Lynn was
placed on a stretcher and, swathed in bandages and surrounded by police, taken to an ambulance. When a reporter ran up and started firing off questions, she simply
pulled the sheet over her head. Wayne Kerr scurried
alongside the stretcher, holding tightly to his briefcase.
The ambulance took Carol Lynn to a waiting private jet
bound for Boston and the renowned Burn Trauma Center
of Massachusetts General. There, the world's leading burn
specialists would begin performing skin grafts on her
back, arms, hands, legs, and the right side of her face and
neck. Plastic surgeons would also labor to reconstruct her
right ear. It had been all but completely seared off in the
blast.

◆ ◆ ◆

Two full days had passed since her death, but Margaret
Benson's legacy lived on. Wayne Kerr and Steven, who
seemed closer buddies than ever since the tragedy, had
met with police resistance when they showed up to take
records from the house—records that investigators hoped
might yield the smoking gun in the case. But that did not
prevent Kerr from acting swiftly in his capacity as Margaret's attorney and filing her will. The will, drawn up by
Kerr and dated May 11, 1983, named Carol Lynn, Steven
and Scott as Margaret's heirs and Kerr as executor and

trustee. Kerr's probable fee was between $500,000 and $750,000. To qualify as executor of the estate under Florida law, however, Kerr had to be a legal resident of the state. He had got around that technicality by filing a declaration of domicile along with the will, listing the Meridian Security trailer as his home address.

The clerk of the Probate Court had some disturbing news for Kerr: A second will, dated January 29, 1985, had just been filed by Naples attorney Guion DeLoach. Within minutes, Kerr was on the phone to Guy DeLoach. An hour later, he and Steven sat in DeLoach's Naples office. Steven was expressionless, but sweat poured off Kerr as DeLoach, silver-haired and unflappable, read the will.

In a bewildering posthumous slap at Kerr, Margaret, having spotted a sign in the window of DeLoach's storefront operation that read "Have you made your will?" had simply walked in and drawn up a new will, specifically excluding Kerr as executor. It was up to the three children to divide the ten million dollars among themselves. Margaret, it seemed, had seen no reason to repay Kerr for his loyalty even when she'd relied on him to protect her from the aberrancies of her son. Kerr questioned the validity of Margaret's signature, but once convinced it was genuine, he began to shudder.

"Calm down," said Steven in an attempt to soothe his pal. "Things will be all right."

But Kerr could hardly be expected to enjoy watching three quarters of a million dollars slip out of reach.

Chapter 32

There were thirty-eight signatures in the guestbook—local people, mostly Steve Benson's fashionable-looking young business acquaintances, who had come to pay their respects at a closed-casket wake in Naples' Pittman Funeral Home.

The dozen or so people who had really known Margaret and Scott sat in a semicircle in the smaller, more private family viewing room. At one end, to the left of the twin coffins, was a large silver coffee urn. There were china cups and plates heaped with cookies. Instead of sharing memories of the dear departed, conversation dwelt on the state of the family business and on the criminal investigation. Brenda Turnbull, a Kleenex in one hand and a cigarette in the other, balanced a cup and saucer in her lap. She was telling Stephen Dancsec, one of Steve Benson's Meridian Security installers, that police had asked her if Steve Benson was "capable of making bombs." Benson, overhearing Turnbull, turned from Debbie and broke into the conversation. "Yes, that's right," he said. "I had made bombs when I was younger—out of copper pipes with gunpowder inside. I exploded them."[*] Then he stood up and went into the main viewing room. More people had come to sign the guestbook. It would be rude not to thank them.

◆ ◆ ◆

On their way to the funeral in Lancaster two days later, Kerr and Steven made a brief side trip to Boston to visit Carol Lynn. When they heard this, Janet Lee Hitchcock Murphy and Harry Hitchcock got on the phone to their lawyer and asked that a guard be put on Carol Lynn—just in case.

Medically, the news was good. Carol Lynn's doctors, encouraged by her remarkable progress, had upgraded their patient's condition from critical to serious. However, they cautioned her to expect many more operations and months, perhaps years, of therapy.

On the afternoon of Sunday, July 14, in Lancaster, police and bouncer-size employees of the Fred F. Groff Funeral Home kept snooping reporters and the morbidly curious away from the black-and-silver Fleetwood limousines that lined Duke Street outside St. James Episcopal Church. More than three hundred people filed into St. James, filling it to capacity. Built in 1744 and the final resting place of several Revolutionary War heroes who served here as vestrymen, the red-brick church stands, with its cloisters and faded granite tombstones, in counterpoint to the modern concrete-and-smoked-glass county courthouse across the street. Faint rays of sunlight pierced the

[*]Turnbull would later testify that she could not recall any such exchange taking place.

stained-glass windows and fell across the blood-red roses blanketing the two seven-thousand-dollar oak coffins.

"Their deaths," intoned Canon Stanley F. Imboden, "were foolish, ugly and reprehensible"—not unlike that of Christ, he continued, a death "that was also calamitous and bewildering. . . . We cannot undo this tragic story. At the moment many of its pages are missing and we can't go back and rewrite them." But, he added, "hard and senseless adversity like the deaths of Margaret and Scott will be redeemed by the hand of God." The Reverend Imboden turned to Kurt and Travis Kendall, Carol Lynn's teenage sons, and offered them his prayers for the recovery of their mother. "It is up to us to bring peace and hope to the living." Both boys, sitting there in the pew alongside Steven and Debbie, bore more than a passing resemblance to Scott.

After the hour-long communion service, Janet Lee helped her father, frail and confused, to a waiting limousine while pallbearers carried the two coffins out of the church and loaded them into hearses. One of Scott's pallbearers was Tom Schelling, the roofer who once saw Steve Benson explode two pipe bombs on the family tennis court. Steve and Debbie brushed by Schelling on their way to the limousines taking them and other family members to Woodward Hill Cemetery. Debbie wore a severe suit and a huge hat that made her look like the proverbial "woman in black."

Shielded from the intense afternoon sun by a lime-green awning, the family sat in stunned silence during the brief tombside service—Harry Hitchcock staring into space, his hands folded in his lap; Janet smiling bravely and occasionally giving her father an affectionate squeeze; and Steven, looking devastated, holding hands with Debbie throughout the service. When it was at last over, each person was given a rose from the coffins. Harry, the lover of flowers turned lover of men, held the rose from his daughter's casket in one hand and reached out to Steven with the other. In the emotion of the moment, he grabbed his grandson's hand and gave it an understanding squeeze. Steven burst into tears.

The following morning, Harry Hitchcock reluctantly picked up the ringing phone at his School Lane Hills house. It was Steven, asking Boppa if he could borrow twenty thousand dollars to tide over the business until the will could be probated. Understanding Harry didn't give it a second thought. Of course he would. Margaret would have wanted it that way.

◆ ◆ ◆

Back at Woodward Hill Cemetery, the names of Margaret and Scott Benson, chiseled on slabs of marble, were placed in the crypt. At the last minute, someone discovered there had been a macabre error. By some curious fluke, the plaques for mother and son had been reversed.

Chapter 33

Agents of the Bureau of Alcohol, Tobacco and Firearms were justifiably proud of the record they'd chalked up since 1970, when Congress empowered the agency to act as a sort of national bomb squad. In the year before the Benson killings alone, they boasted forty-nine convictions to just four acquittals. Out of more than 280 other bombings in that same period, ATF investigators did the legwork that led to two hundred–plus indictments. They accomplished this by simply declaring war on bombers.

The case before them was no exception. To find the killer or killers of Margaret and Scott Benson, an even dozen men and women from ATF—explosives technicians, chemists, physicists, auditors, fingerprint authorities, experts of every conceivable stripe—would work full-time on the case for forty-four days before claiming victory.

For George Nowicki, Tommy Nolle and Terry Hopkins, the first ATF agents at the scene, the two blackened craters beneath the twisted skeleton of the Suburban left no doubt as to where the bombs had been placed—one in the console between Scott and his mother, the other directly under the seat in which Carol Lynn had been sitting. That Tuesday afternoon, Al Gleason, a basset-faced ATF enforcement officer with forty years' experience under his belt, stood in the Benson driveway looking at a jagged fragment of metal, by his reckoning the remains of a four-inch pipe end cap. It bore a telltale initial—a tiny ''U'' that would lead to the manufacturer, and then to local stores where it and other parts of the bomb might have been purchased.

The shredded, bloodstained clothes Margaret and Scott wore that fatal day were packed into three green-and-white Sta-Nu paint cans. Steven's clothes were stuffed into a plain brown paper bag. They were among the seventy-eight separately tagged pieces of evidence—tiny fragments of galvanized metal, splinters, cotton swabs dabbed with unidentified material cleaned off the bodies themselves—turned over to senior chemist Walter Mitchell for analysis at ATF's Atlanta laboratory. His wire-rimmed spectacles, mussed gray hair and slight twitch made Mitchell, a twenty-year ATF veteran, look every bit the tweedy scientist.

No sooner had the samples arrived in his lab, filled with lasers, microscopes and X-ray equipment, than Mitchell pulled the clothes from the paint cans and examined them visually for any foreign particles, however tiny, that might yield clues. Using a process known as thin-layer chromatography, Mitchell then shaved a wafer-thin slice off each bit of evidence, treated it chemically and placed it in an ultraviolet cabinet. In this strangely beautiful purple-black light, there showed up clearly under the microscope tiny flecks of smokeless gunpowder, the kind used in shotgun shells.

There were, in fact, traces of the gunpowder that had been used in the pipe bombs on virtually every piece of evidence. Mitchell was not surprised. The size of the blast was so tremendous, gunpowder would have showed up on anyone or anything within a considerable radius—twenty feet, at least. It was curious, then, that there were no traces of powder on Steve's clothing.

Something else caught Mitchell's trained eye, though—a tiny metal particle on the right leg of Steve's jeans, which had gone unnoticed. Mitchell picked off the barely visible flake with a pair of tweezers and examined it. The metal substance turned out to be zinc. Mitchell had also scraped some white powder off one of the galvanized pipe fragments, and he discovered, after chemical analysis, that it was zinc oxide. The zinc could not have been blown onto Steve Benson's pants leg without traces of gunpowder, however infinitesimal, showing up too. The zinc could have rubbed off the pipe onto Benson's pants. But when?

◆ ◆ ◆

It came as a surprise to Lieutenant Harold Young, coming just eight days after the crime. Steven Benson's lawyer, Thomas Biggs, was telling the police that his client was not available for questions "anymore, any longer or ever again." When reporters called, Lieutenant Young shrugged that off. It was a citizen's constitutional right not to answer questions, he told the papers, and besides, "it doesn't destroy our investigation or anything." Steven Benson, Young hastened to add, was not even a suspect. Steven called Harry Hitchcock to explain that he was refusing to cooperate only on advice of counsel. The old man understood. Letting lawyers speak for you was just standard operating procedure, wasn't it?

◆ ◆ ◆

Right now, Young and the boys from ATF were more interested in what Wayne Kerr could provide. They obtained a subpoena ordering him to turn over all the files on family businesses, bank accounts, real estate holdings, the lot. What Steven wouldn't tell them, the financial records surely would.

Kerr was too preoccupied to put up much of a fight. He had initial reservations that as Mrs. Benson's lawyer, he might be violating some lawyer-client privilege. But right now he was mulling over his strategy for challenging the second will, which removed him as executor. Coming up with a cogent plan would not be easy. Kerr was finding it increasingly difficult to concentrate. The magnitude of the tragedy was just beginning to sink in during that first week after the bombing. The mere notion of starting up a car terrified him; Kerr would sit behind the wheel for what seemed like an eternity, trying to summon the courage to turn the key. The sleepless nights weren't helping, either. The bombing scene played over and over again in his mind, only in his dreams the victims weren't Margaret and Scott but his own loved ones. Kerr would sit bolt upright in bed, his pulse pounding, the sheets soaked with sweat. He prayed the nightmare would go away.

For Harry Hitchcock, the nightmare would never go away: it was his reality. In the days after the disaster, he sat at home staring out the window, trying to make sense of it. His world was crumbling around him, but he soon discovered he was not grieving alone. Mail from well-wishers, many of whom he had never met, poured into the house on Center Street. "Dear Uncle Harry," wrote a seven-year-old girl from nearby Millersville. "I am praying for you I will pray to God to heal your heart." A ninety-one-year-old woman who, like thousands of others, had been a springtime pilgrim to Harry's garden, wrote asking if he "knew the joy you have given thousands of people through the years? And now, to think that you, who have given pleasure to so many, should experience the pain of a real tragedy."

The letters helped, but Harry leaned hardest on his steadfast Christian faith. The Sunday after the murders, while praying with a friend, he even blurted out forgiveness for the killers of his daughter and grandson. "I have a Lord of forgiveness," he said. "The Lord has forgiven me. . . . I have no alternative but to forgive whoever in his sick mind did this act that I can't understand. . . . Jesus Christ is suffering with me. I know the Lord is going through this with me." There could be no greater test of his Christian faith, Harry knew, than to have had his daughter killed this way.

Chapter 34

Diana Galloway's Maserati-red fingernails flew back and forth across the yellow legal pad as she scribbled her calculations in pencil—she sometimes preferred the old-fashioned way to punching the buttons on a calculator. Arrows and lines connected boxes with circles and circles with circles and boxes with other boxes, as if a corporate organization chart had been superimposed over the game plan of a demented football coach. Galloway, an attractive fortyish blonde with a languid Blanche DuBois drawl, had been sifting through the chaotic financial affairs of Meridian and the Bensons for days. Cardboard boxes brimming with invoices, receipts, bank statements, mortgage records, loan documents, checkbooks, canceled checks, IRS returns, and checkbook registers were at Galloway's feet, an Everest of numbers was atop her desk. As one of the ATF's most capable auditors, Galloway loved the Sherlock Holmes adventure of it all—puzzling out the financial dealings and misdealings of suspected criminals, using logic alone to nail an embezzler, to find the motive for arson. Or for murder.

This particular Rubik's Cube was finally getting to Galloway, not because she was unable to uncover irregularities in the books—Steven Benson's repeated use of counter checks made out to cash instead of recorded, numbered checks to supposedly cover business expenses was an immediate red flag—but because the irregularities were extensive. Meridian's records were so sloppy, in fact, that she worried she might never be able to track down the huge sums that flowed from Margaret.

Galloway would eventually, after months of sleuthing, discover that between May 1984 and the day of the bombing, $247,130.27 was funneled from Margaret's personal account to Meridian and eventually into Steve Benson's account. After writing checks to cover legitimate business expenses, he pocketed a tidy sum: $112,192.43.

Before she got even close to arriving at these final figures, Galloway found one of the two blank checks Margaret had signed, to cover a few incidental business expenses, before she left for Europe. Steven had made it out for $50,000 and deposited the money into the Meridian Security account. From that he withdrew $25,000, put it in his personal checking account and made out another check, a cashier's check, for $23,797.03—the down payment on the $235,000 dream house in Brynwood.

❖ ❖ ❖

There was no point in even trying to make out the signatures on the two invoices ATF agent Terry Hopkins had uncovered at Hughes Supply. Obviously, they were not meant to be deciphered. Enter Frank Kendall, the agency's craggy-faced, bearded answer to Commander Whitehead. Just months from retirement, after twenty-four years, Kendall was considered perhaps the agency's best fingerprint man, with hundreds of thousands of identifications to his credit.

The wrinkled, dog-eared invoices presented a special problem. Employing a special chemical process developed by the agency, Kendall managed only to lift off a single, barely usable fingerprint. The process yielded an unexpected bonus, however: two clear left palm prints, impressions made where the writer's hand touched the surface of the paper as he scrawled the signature. Like fingerprints, no two palm prints are identical.

Kendall was given only one set of prints to compare with the prints he'd found on the invoices. Even a naked-eye examination left no doubt in his mind—the fingerprint on the invoice from Hughes Supply did not match any of the set obtained by the Collier County Sheriff's Department. It wasn't even close.

The palm prints were another matter. Carefully, meticulously, he examined the latticework of loops and swirls, marking each point of similarity. When he had finished, he tallied them: sixty matching traits, three times as many as were necessary to conclude that the palm prints of the person who bought the end caps that may have been used to kill Margaret and Scott and this set of prints belonged to the same person.

They belonged to Steven Benson.

Chapter 35

Steve's soothing words concerning the two wills were not enough to placate Wayne Kerr. They were still buddies, but Kerr knew that where money was involved, friendship meant little. Wayne had been closest to Margaret, impressed by her warmth, her class—and she had led him to believe that she had a genuine affection for him. Even Harry Hitchcock was bewildered by Margaret's apparent change of heart. She trusted Kerr completely, Harry had thought. Yet the second will proved that even to Margaret, Kerr was in the final analysis another hired hand. Expendable.

There was really no logical reason why Steven, despite his reassurances, would act any differently. By excluding Kerr as executor and dividing up the spoils themselves, Steve and Carol Lynn would save themselves as much as $750,000—$375,000 apiece. Even though Margaret left all her jewelry to Carol Lynn in the 1983 will, Mother's baubles (worth considerably less than $375,000) would not make it worth Carol Lynn's while to contest the new will.

Kerr walked into the Naples office of Dean Witter Reynolds and asked for an even one million dollars in stocks from Margaret's account. Broker John Melick asked Kerr to take a seat and went into another office to make a phone call. Melick had been told about the two wills, but he also knew that Kerr had been Margaret's lawyer and legal confidant. He called the Collier County Courthouse and asked for a judge's opinion on what to do. Nothing, Melick was told. The funds were to stay put. Kerr lumbered out of the Dean Witter Reynolds offices empty-handed.

His actions flung open a Pandora's box of protests from his colleagues. Lancaster lawyer Jack Hartman, attorney for the Hitchcock and Benson families since the 1950s and the administrator of both Edward Benson's trust and Charlotte Hitchcock's estate, thought it improper that Kerr named himself executor of the 1983 will in the first place; he hadn't anticipated this latest move. Guy DeLoach was outraged. "To me as a member of the bar," DeLoach said when he heard of Kerr's failed maneuver, "to stand back and watch this guy try to do that . . . is just too much. Technically, there is nothing to prevent Kerr from liquidating the assets of that estate."

Determined to do something about it, DeLoach turned to fellow Naples lawyer Donald Van Koughnet—who three decades before had been a co-prosecutor in the Alger Hiss spy case—to draw up a legal memorandum seeking final revocation of the troublesome 1983 will. On July 29, Van Koughnet fired the opening salvo, charging before Collier County Judge Charles T. Carlton that Margaret Benson never properly signed the 1983 will and that Kerr might have been guilty of fraud and perjury when he professed to the probate court judge that he was unaware of any will written after 1983. "I think the whole circum-

stances of the whole matter," said Von Koughnet, "are
extremely suspect."

Through his own lawyer, William Blackwell, Kerr shot back that he "knew nothing of the second will and did his duty by filing the first one." Kerr demanded nothing from the Dean Witter Reynolds brokers; he merely "asked for what was due him." After listening to Van Koughnet, Judge Carlton ordered that the entire estate be frozen until the issue of the two wills was resolved. For Steve Benson, Carlton's ruling meant that he could no longer dip into Mother's coffers to keep his business afloat. As of August 1, 1985, the Meridian network ceased to exist.

Chapter 36

The woman looking back at her as she held up the mirror no longer had the porcelain-perfect complexion of Grace Kelly; the skin stretched from below her right cheekbone to the base of her neck like a dime-store Halloween mask. Yet her right ear had been masterfully restored, the extensive grafts on her hands and legs had taken, and Carol Lynn had to be thankful that she was alive at all.

There was still pain, excruciating, agonizing pain. The patient had to force herself to go through the torture of turning her neck sideways rather than avoid the discomfort altogether by just pivoting her entire body. The skin would never regain its elasticity otherwise; she was still going through endless hours of exercise to regain the mobility in her hands and right arm. The grafted skin also reacted to changes in the weather; when the barometer dropped, her skin tightened painfully.

They wanted to know if she was ready to go out, how she felt about being seen in public. Carol Lynn was no longer a beauty queen, but then she knew better than anyone that she hadn't been one for some time. She was eager to get back to her home in Chestnut Hill near Brookline, and to get on with the business of dividing up Mother's estate. On August 5, Carol Lynn and Steven each asked the Collier County Probate Court to be appointed as administrators of Margaret's 1985 will, effectively squeezing Kerr out of the picture once and for all. Five days later, Carol Lynn was released from Mass. General, her features hidden beneath hat, scarf and sunglasses as she was pushed in a wheelchair to the front door of the hospital.

Carol Lynn was eager to get back to work on her thesis—the script for a spy thriller. She hoped to sell it to Hollywood, but barring that, she thought of producing it herself, and having the movie serve as her doctoral dissertation. She had barely settled back in with Kurt and Travis when, the following Tuesday, she received a call from Carl Westman, the lawyer now representing her interests in Naples. Collier County Circuit Court Judge Hugh Hayes had appointed Westman interim representative of the Benson estate. Carol Lynn, not Steven and certainly not Wayne Kerr, would control the estate. She had to wonder why the judge seemed so unsympathetic to her brother and why the court excluded him outright. Surely whoever killed Margaret and Scott had also hurt Steven deeply.

Chapter 37

"**W**hy in the hell would my grandfather, an Italian immigrant hod carrier who lived in New York for twenty-five years and worked on Grant's Tomb, suddenly pick up in his late forties and move to Fort Myers, Florida? Because he was going to buy a farm in Fort Myers, *Virginia*, and got on the wrong train. Grandpa didn't speak much English."

For Joe D'Alessandro, the path to becoming a Florida state attorney and one of the country's top prosecutors was no less circuitous. A Fort Meyers native ("We were the only Roman Catholics in town back then"), D'Alessandro went to live with relatives in Brooklyn when he was eleven and soon got involved with a street gang. Dad, a would-be pharmacist who had wound up owning a bar, hauled his delinquent son back to Florida and stuck him in St. Leo's, a parochial school run by Benedictine monks.

A journalism major in Florida, D'Alessandro ("Mr. D" to his fanatically loyal staff) fell in love with the law while researching a paper on John Peter Zenger, the eighteenth-century journalist and printer, whose trial for libel advanced the cause of freedom of the press in America. Rejected by the University of Florida's law school, D'Alessandro applied instead to Stetson University in De Land. (Years later, when he was chairman of the criminal division of the Florida bar and attending a bar association meeting at Disney World, D'Alessandro boarded the monorail at 6:30 A.M. and realized that the only other passenger was the University of Florida law school dean who had rejected his application. The dean's face dropped when D'Alessandro, by then one of the best-known legal figures in the state, reminded him of the incident. "Ah, sweet revenge," says D'Alessandro, his blue eyes lighting up as he taps another cigarette out of an ever-present pack of Merits). Mr. D likes to recall that he passed the bar exam on the same day he was sworn into the army—June 4, 1964.

Even before the governor appointed him state attorney only five years later, the stocky prosecutor had gained a reputation for toughness. He was a hard plea bargainer because he couldn't wait to get back in the courtroom to do battle. "I love," he liked to say, "the Me versus You of it."

He had plenty of opportunity for the "Me versus You" in southwest Florida, where extremes of affluence and poverty mixed with drugs to produce a hyperactive criminal subculture. D'Alessandro had almost become accustomed to the rapists, homicidal drug dealers, child molesters and serial killers who paraded through the courtrooms of Lee, Collier and Charlotte counties.

Still, nothing had prepared him for what happened one evening in 1983, when Bonnie Kelly, whose boyfriend was standing trial on drug charges, gunned down Assistant

State Attorney Eugene Berry as he stood outside the front door of his Charlotte County home. Berry had been D'Alessandro's deputy and his close friend. He undertook Bonnie Kelly's prosecution as a personal mission, convincing a jury to convict her of first-degree murder.

Kelly might have gone to Florida's much-used electric chair, had it not been for Michael McDonnell. Every bit as flamboyant as Joe D'Alessandro was tough, McDonnell fancied himself something of an updated Sunbelt version of F. Lee Bailey, in his exquisitely tailored suits, lizard-skin boots with inch-and-a-half heels, and gold-rimmed aviator shades. He could be seen talking on the car phone while driving his white Jaguar to the club. He was Hollywood handsome. He had a granite jaw, a blinding tooth-polish smile and styled hair with just enough silver to lend that distinguished touch. He had a radio announcer's voice. He made, it was estimated, $500,000 a year. He was, his clients would tell you, worth the price.

McDonnell, born in Paterson, New Jersey, and raised outside Detroit, was a high school jock who graduated from West Point in 1962 and went on to serve two tours of duty as an infantry captain in Vietnam. A Stetson alumnus like D'Alessandro, he quickly built a reputation for himself on the opposite side of the courtroom aisle. In 1975, he took on the defense of a Naples man accused of murdering the widow of a former Michigan attorney general. The jury in that case took only twenty minutes to render its not-guilty verdict.

McDonnell's professional intensity may have taken its toll on his personal life. When his first marriage broke up, he took a year off to write a novel and tour as a country-western singer ("I had to recharge my battery"). Now, in his mid-forties, he seemed to have everything: a striking

168

second wife and a beautiful young family, all the trappings
of success and the standing that went with it. But he had
never had that really big case, the case that would make
the headlines nationwide, that would be talked about by
Roger Mudd and Dan Rather and Tom Brokaw on the
evening news, then rehashed by Ted Koppel and again
the next morning on *Today*. That would make *60 Minutes*.
That would make McDonnell as familiar a name to informed Americans as Bailey, Belli, Nizer, Williams and
Dershowitz. That would make Michael McDonnell a real
legal eagle.

Until now. The rumors had already been flying for
weeks when McDonnell was first approached to represent
Steven Benson. Things were not looking good. The evidence, circumstantial as it may have seemed, was pointing
to one person—Steve Benson. McDonnell had in the past
few years built up a sizable civil caseload and now made
it a practice to take on only the rare criminal case. If an
indictment was forthcoming, Benson would be charged
with blowing up his own mother, brother and sister for
one of the great tobacco fortunes.

It didn't get much rarer than this.

Chapter 38

**STEVEN BENSON ARRESTED
SON OF LOCAL HEIRESS IS
CHARGED WITH BOMB MURDER
OF HIS MOTHER, BROTHER**

*He Set 2 Bombs on Morning
Trip to Store, Agents Say*

By Ernest Schreiber and Ad Crable
New Era Staff Writers

NAPLES, Fla.—Steven Wayne Benson, heir to a multi-million-dollar Lancaster tobacco fortune, was arrested at a Fort Myers, Fla., business today and charged with the July 9 car bomb murder of his mother and brother in Florida.

◆ ◆ ◆

The story went on to reveal the charges: two counts of first-degree murder and one count of attempted first-degree murder. It described how Steven had filled two steel

170

pipe cannisters with gunpowder, then planted them in the family car underneath the seats, while his mother, brother and sister were still inside the house, and reported that Steven was being held without bail.

◆ ◆ ◆

He had known it was coming, but not exactly when or where. That morning, Benson had driven to the Fort Myers law offices of Woldorf, Kiesel and Hillmyer to talk to Debbie's lawyer, Barry Hillmyer, presumably about the guardianship of his children should an arrest take place. He had been there only a few minutes when, at precisely 10:00 A.M. on August 22, Lieutenant Young and ATF agent George Nowicki walked in and placed Steve Benson under arrest. He registered no emotion, and spoke only to complain that the yellow Thunderbird transporting him to the Collier County jail was "kind of small."

The scene, aired on television stations in Florida and Pennsylvania, would be indelibly etched in the minds of millions: Benson, looking sullen and chunky in navy-blue slacks and a light-gray short-sleeved shirt, being led into the jail with his hands cuffed in front of him. Later, inside the jail, he was given one of the bright-orange jumpsuits worn by all inmates, and put in a cellblock with three other new prisoners, by way of indoctrination to jail life. Once settled, he ordered eggs Benedict for lunch.

Kurt Kendall heard news of his uncle's arrest on the radio and called his mother at home. Carol Lynn's hospital bed depositions at both Naples Community Hospital and Massachusetts General constituted some of the most damning evidence against Steven, yet through her attorney, Ric Cirace, she professed shock at the arrest. "She had no idea," Cirace, a short, stocky Boston lawyer with a fondness for gold jewelry and a tanning-booth glow, told reporters. "It's another of a series of tragedies that have befallen her family."

For Harry Hitchcock, the "what ifs" had been piling up for seven weeks—what if Margaret had stayed longer with Carol Lynn in Massachusetts, what if Harry and Janet had invited her to come up for a seashore holiday in Maryland in July instead of August? It was time Boppa got on with what little was probably left of his life, Janet thought. She insisted on going ahead with their plans to vacation at Ocean City, Maryland, and that is where they were when they heard the news. Janet was not surprised; to her, Steven had always seemed cold and distant, far more interested in material things than any of her children. But then she remembered how her sister Margaret had spoiled Carol Lynn, Steven and Scott, and those Christmases when it took all day for the Benson kids to open their presents. Then there was Debbie. If Steven had always been aloof, at least he was devoted to his mother, a loving son—until Debbie came along.

No one, not even Carol Lynn, suffered more from the reality of Steven's arrest than Harry. The news came as a head-spinning shock, not because he was hopelessly naive—Hitchcock had not built his fortune by being an innocent—or because he was in his dotage. Hitchcock, though fragile physically, retained a clarity of wit and a depth of insight into the human condition that were not available to most men half his age. His grandson's arrest came as an emotional blow because it forced Harry to face what in his heart he had long feared: His spiritual rebirth had come in time to save him but too late to save his flesh and blood.

At first, Harry refused to believe it. "He is innocent

172

until proven guilty," he told a *New Era* reporter. "I pray
and pray that he is innocent." Carol Lynn held out little
hope for her brother's innocence, but she did have some
happy news for her grandfather: She, too, was now a
born-again Christian. "I owe it all to the Lord," she told
him, "that I'm still alive."

◆ ◆ ◆

On the morning of Friday, August 23, Michael McDonnell
filed a written plea of not guilty to all charges and demanded that a bail hearing be set. At precisely the same
time that Steve Benson was placed under a round-the-
clock suicide watch in maximum security, moving men
were carting out the last few pieces of his mother's furniture from 1515 Ridge Road, the house where Margaret
Benson had raised her loving children.

Chapter 39

The press conference was—as McDonnell had hoped it would be—packed. Pushing back his glasses and clearing his throat, he read his client's statement *con brio*. " 'I am frustrated and angry over a crime I did not commit,' " McDonnell intoned. " 'This is a terrible ordeal for my family and me, but I am confident we have the strength to make it through. I am anguished for the suffering of my children and my wife and wish desperately that I might be reunited with them.' "

This news conference was an opening salvo in McDonnell's fight to get Steven Benson out on bail, and he was not about to stop with the statement. He took this opportunity to slam the prosecution for allegations that Benson had embezzled two million dollars from Margaret and that she had in fact called Wayne Kerr down to Florida to cut her son out of the will. Even Kerr, who was still refusing to give a deposition to the prosecution because he was wary of violating his lawyer-client relationship with the Benson clan, openly admitted this was untrue. If he had been called down to cut Steven out of the will, Kerr said, wouldn't he at least have brought the will with him? Answering this question must have been especially galling to Kerr; after all, the person Margaret Benson cut out of her will was Wayne Kerr.

There was another sore point with McDonnell—the widely trumpeted speculation on the part of D'Alessandro that Steven had systematically embezzled two million dollars from his mother. According to one of Carol Lynn's sworn statements to the police, Margaret had once tossed off the two-million-dollar figure. Here, the state was winging it. Until ATF auditor Diana Galloway could come back to them with the final word on just how much of his mother's money Steven may have absconded with, the best they could do was go with the dead woman's own estimate.

None of these allegations worried the defense as much as did the rumored existence of a telltale fingerprint on a supply company invoice. "I'm just wondering," McDonnell's associate and co-counsel Jerry Berry told a local newspaper, "if next week we will be here explaining the fingerprint doesn't exist." (Indeed, a matching *fingerprint* did not.)

◆ ◆ ◆

The largest criminal investigation in Collier County history paid off for the ATF and D'Alessandro's team September 6, when the grand jury handed down nine indictments against Steve Benson: the first-degree murders of Margaret and Scott; the attempted murder of Carol Lynn; "making, possessing and discharging destructive devices" resulting in the death of Margaret and Scott; arson; arson "resulting

175

in great bodily harm" to Margaret, Scott and Carol Lynn. The first two of the charges carried with them a maximum penalty of death.

It had been a grand slam for the state, but it would still be ten full months before Benson would be brought to trial—months of legal maneuvering, sparring in the press and, not incidentally, jockeying for control of Benson millions.

From the outset, it would be an uphill battle for McDonnell on all fronts. After the indictments came down, Harry had at Janet's urging opened his mind to the horrifying possibility that Steven might actually have done it. If Steven had, then Harry, Janet and Carol Lynn still stood between him and additional millions. With all three out of the way, he might fall heir to $100 million or more (press reports were already inflating the figure to $400 million). As Janet scoured the newspapers, she was alarmed to come across reports that Steve might actually get out on bail. A dozen letters had been written to Circuit Court Judge Hugh Hayes on Steve's behalf, and McDonnell grew so confident that he did not even bother to call any character witnesses to testify at the bail hearing.

Harry, still a devout believer in the direct approach, placed a call to Judge Hayes, only to be told by his secretary that His Honor was "unavailable." So Harry sat down at his desk and, pausing only to look up at a framed photograph of Margaret, drafted an urgent plea to Hayes. Janet wrote a letter of her own, and dispatched them both by Federal Express. They landed on the judge's desk the next morning.

"Anyone who is capable of murdering his mother for money is capable of murdering his grandfather for the same reason," wrote Harry. "I am concerned and alarmed

. . . afraid for my own safety and the safety of my grand-
daughter Carol Lynn." Janet agreed that since Carol Lynn
was shaping up to be the star witness against Steven, she
could be in grave danger if her brother was released. "I
beg you," Janet wrote, "not to set bail." Janet's younger,
married daughter, Sheryl Murray, added her voice to the
chorus of noes. "I know my cousin very well," she wrote.
"I know what a callous, cold man he is. . . . I would not
sleep nights knowing he was free."

Harry stopped short of stating flat out that Steven was
guilty, but that was cold comfort to the defense team. One
week later, Judge Hayes, pointing out that Debbie was the
only family member who seemed not to oppose freeing
Steven, denied bail. "The state has met its burden," he
ruled. "The proof of guilt is evident and the presumption
is great."

In Lancaster, the *Intelligencer-Journal* left little doubt as
to where the hometown press stood on the issue of Benson's probable guilt. "We have long been taught that all
persons accused of crimes must be considered innocent
until proven guilty," read the next day's editorial. "So be
it. But we would be naive to ignore the fact there is a very
strong presumption that police officials did not err in ar-
resting Steven Benson for this crime. Steven Benson will
have his day in court. His guilt or innocence will be decided by his peers. But this crime is so heinous—the work
of a warped mind—that it would have been totally irresponsible to permit the person suspected of committing it
to be free while awaiting trial. Regardless of the outcome
of Steven Benson's trial, Judge Hayes did exactly what he
had to do under the circumstances, and we respect him
for it."

Harry, Janet and Carol Lynn breathed a collective sigh

of relief. "I think it's safer for us and for him," said Harry of his grandson, "to stay where he is right now." Back in his Naples jail cell, Steven pulled at the waistband of his prisoner's orange jumpsuit. He was losing weight fast.

Chapter 40

Daddy had been behind bars for more than two months, and the bills were piling up. Without the usual infusions of cash from Margaret, Debbie found herself trying to cope with a steadily mounting stack of bills. Under Florida's "Slayer Statute," anyone convicted of murder cannot inherit from the victim. It remained to be seen—if Steven was ultimately found guilty—whether his portion of Margaret's bequest might bypass him and go straight to his three small children, with Debbie as trustee.

Carol Lynn would certainly do everything in her power to stop this; she remembered her mother's words that under no circumstances did she want Debbie to get her hands on so much as "a grain of sand." But Carol Lynn could do nothing about the kids' $220,000 trust fund, and on September 30, the Lee County Circuit Court ruled that Debbie could dip into the trust fund and withdraw $5,969—enough to meet two months' worth of mortgage and auto payments.

✦ ✦ ✦

Brynwood had stringent deed restrictions, so Debbie had to go outside her exclusive little enclave to find the right locale for what she had in mind. Her friend Leo Robinson did not hesitate to lend her the space she needed. This was something people in the Robinsons' part of Fort Myers did all the time. On a balmy autumn weekend, the wife of the Lancaster Leaf tobacco heir staged a tag sale in her friends' garage to sell the children's old cribs, stuffed animals and other toys, along with some dishes. She collected five hundred dollars.

Chapter 41

The thunderhead that had dumped a half inch of rain on North Naples in less than an hour this September afternoon had just begun to pass slowly to the south when a squad car pulled over to a battered pickup with suspicious-looking cargo. The shiny metal canister had some kind of push-button control panel affixed to it, and if the two police officers had been told the strange-looking device came from outer space, it could not have shocked them more than the truth did. This was, in fact, a partially assembled nuclear bomb. All it needed was the plutonium to set it off.

They brought Guido Dal Molin, the driver of the pickup and the brains behind the bomb, into the station for questioning. Dal Molin was small and wiry, with long straight hair and a piercing, Rasputin-like stare. This was not the first time the authorities had encountered Dal Molin's electronic wizardry. A few years before, his frantic neighbors called to report a driverless car on the loose. When police stopped the Trans Am, they found Dal Molin in the back seat, driving it with an ingenious remote-control joystick of his own design. As they did then, the police let Dal Molin off this time with a warning.

Pranks notwithstanding, Dal Molin had shown promise as early as age ten, when he could draw electrical wiring diagrams with tremendous accuracy. He was barely out of high school when John Ratliff, founder of Tandy Computers, spotted the prodigy. He was "brilliant and unique," said Ratliff, who had promptly put Dal Molin on the payroll as a researcher. His starting salary was $1,500 a week.

There was a dark side to Dal Molin's genius. He was deep into the drug world, and he had known Scott Benson. Not long after he had been stopped for tooling around town with the homemade atom bomb, two scruffy young men turned up uninvited at his front door early one morning, apparently to collect on a drug deal. Dal Molin burst out of the house with a pistol and began firing wildly. Nobody, he shouted, bothered him that early in the morning. Nobody.

If the defense wanted to show that there were other possible suspects out there with the ability and the inclination to blow up a car in which Scott sat, McDonnell could not have hoped for a better candidate than Naples' own mad electronics genius.

PART FOUR

THE
TRIAL

"Scott could be a miserable SOB if he had to."

—CAROL LYNN KENDALL
TO THE AUTHORITIES,
RIGHT AFTER THE BOMBING

"I can't see any reason why anyone would want to kill Margaret Benson. I see a lot of reasons why somebody would want to kill Scott."

—PAUL HARVEY,
CAPTAIN OF THE *GALLEON QUEEN*

Chapter 42

It was inevitable that it would come out, but what did it matter now? Scotty was beyond hurting. Carol Lynn had been told by her own attorney, Ric Cirace, not to shrink from answering any question McDonnell might throw at her during the deposition, no matter how embarrassing it was. He would be testing her credibility under oath, and even the whitest of lies might give McDonnell the ammunition he needed to sink the case against Steven.

What little air there was in the windowless conference room at the Collier County Courthouse—neutral turf—seemed to vanish as McDonnell hammered away. The line of questioning was artfully oblique. Was this stay at Massachusetts General for the treatment of her injuries the only time she had been to the hospital? No. Then when and where? Carol Lynn admitted that as a teenager she had been admitted to a hospital in Baltimore, to give birth to an out-of-wedlock son: Scott.

What had long been an open secret in Lancaster was,

as Carol Lynn well knew, about to be trumpeted in headlines across the country. Before that could happen, she told Kurt and Travis that their dead uncle had actually been their half-brother. It seemed bitterly ironic, in the torrent of sensationalism this revelation would release, that the only person who had never known, never would know, was Scott himself.

◆ ◆ ◆

Scott was Steven's key out of his jail cell, or so McDonnell was coming to believe. Even the state's witnesses were in unanimous agreement: Steve seemed to be straight and levelheaded, if somewhat humorless and materialistic, and in his own way had been devoted to his mother. Scott, on the other hand, was seen by practically everyone with whom he came in contact as a spoiled, often violent druggie. Carol Lynn and Margaret were afraid of him, and they had every reason to be. If he had crossed one of his unsavory friends in a drug deal, Scott would not have been the first in recent memory to pay the ultimate price, perhaps taking some innocent bystander with him. In Florida, such rubouts, whether by the mob or by an unforgiving independent, had become nothing less than routine. By shifting the spotlight to dead Scotty, McDonnell could cast at least a shadow of a doubt over the prosecution's case. That would be his strategy.

Or at least part of it. Arguing that all the tawdry publicity surrounding the case would make it impossible to pick an impartial jury, McDonnell moved repeatedly for a change of venue. And for a change of judge. Hugh Hayes, McDonnell argued, had signed the original arrest warrant for Steve Benson, and should therefore step down as trial judge in the case.

It would not be that easy. At the age of thirty-eight, the boyish-faced Hayes had been a judge for eight years, and had earned a reputation as one of the smartest, toughest and most ambitious jurists in the state. He was vocal in his support of victim compensation, and for harsher penalties for violent crimes. He had sentenced men to death.

Hayes had a courtroom pallor that at times made him look almost translucent under the glaring overhead lights, and he spoke from the bench with the soft, deliberate southern gentleman accent of a North Carolina native. But the compact five-foot-seven-inch onetime high school jock kept himself in good enough shape to jump into the fray— quite literally. Once, when a prisoner tried to make a run for it, Hayes leapt down from the bench and tackled him, as startled spectators looked on. On a different occasion, a man who attacked his ex-wife in court found himself unexpectedly being pried off her by the judge.

Hayes, who wore custom-made monogrammed shirts, wasn't much easier on lawyers, particularly when it came to delays. The judge did not try to disguise that he was a young man in a hurry; during testimony he was a veritable grab bag of nervous tics, swiveling back and forth in his high-back black leather chair, twirling his pen in his mouth, drumming his fingers on the desktop—all the while maintaining the perfect poker face. He was eager to get on with it, and when prosecutors came before him asking for postponements, he was unforgiving. Trials would proceed on schedule in his courtroom, Hayes warned both sides, "whether you guys are ready or not."

McDonnell would get nowhere trying to prod Hayes

into stepping down, but the judge did take steps to free money for Benson's defense. Because the estate and all the trust funds were now tied up in litigation, at one point Hayes ruled that the millionaire was indigent so that the cost of his defense would be carried by the state. A month later, at some considerable embarrassment, Hayes would reverse himself. Apparently no longer considered indigent, Steven, Hayes then decreed, would be permitted to use $244,974.39 from Margaret's estate to cover his legal expenses. Carol Lynn also was granted her $244,974.39 share.

(By now, dozens of attorneys had become involved as thirty-four claims, totaling $750,000, were filed against the ten-million-dollar estate. Carol Lynn had also filed a $400,000 suit for "medical bills, pain and suffering" against her dead mother's estate. She demanded a $131,000 loan that had been promised her prior to the bombings. In even more bizarre legal maneuvers, Margaret would sue Scott posthumously for $263,856.30, and lawyers for Margaret's estate carted Kim Beegle into court to retrieve Buck, the watchdog Kim insisted Scotty had given to her. Buck, Carol Lynn's lawyers argued, belonged to Scott's estate and therefore was needed as part of the "inventory process" to distribute the estate. Margaret won, and during a hearing in Naples, Kim tearfully surrendered Buck to become part of Margaret Benson's inventory.)

Throughout the spring, McDonnell kept the pressure on Hayes to step down—going so far as to threaten that the judge might be called as a defense witness to prove that the original search and arrest warrants in the case were improperly issued. Hayes would not be budged. And the Holmesian jurist in him was becoming increasingly agitated at the mounting crescendo of publicity— none of which was going to help chances for finding an impartial jury in this part of the state. The solution, it seemed to Hayes, was simply to shut everybody up. It would not be so simple. Hayes' gag order was eventually thrown out by the Florida Second District Court of Appeals. During the time it was in effect, Benson-watchers who were deprived of any hard news got to hear of a projected movie on the case, imaginatively titled *The Benson Pipe-Bomb Murders*. The producer's only other moviemaking credit was, fittingly, *The Amityville Horror*.

News of the plans for a movie prompted five fifth graders from Lancaster's Leola Elementary School to write a letter to the editor. "The incident was bad enough at the time," they protested. "It doesn't need to be repeated."

Chapter 43

Faces streaked with sweat, the grim-faced men in combat fatigues silently make their way under fences and through the tropical underbrush until, without being detected, they arrive at their target destination. A reprise of Vietnam, perhaps, or a behind-the-scenes look at terrorist commandos? No, the jumpy, homemade black-and-white video showed McDonnell's own private detectives easily stealing past Quail Creek's crackerjack private police force, right to the doorstep of 13002 White Violet Drive—proving, as McDonnell would argue, that anyone could have penetrated the community's security to place the deadly devices that killed Margaret and Scott Benson. Of course, Buck was no longer on the premises to greet the intruders, and the question still remained how these mysterious suspects could have planted the bombs in the Suburban the night before without setting off the canine alarm system.

Still, McDonnell was pleased with the job Bob Laws had done producing and directing *Rambo III*, as the pecu-

liar tape came to be known. A beefy, red-faced veteran of
twenty-seven years in law enforcement—nine of them in
homicide—Miami-based Laws seemed every inch the typ-
ical Florida cop. After his retirement in 1984, the aptly
named Laws had banded together with two other retirees
to set up their own P.I. firm, Proteus International. Proteus was already doing a brisk divorce and corporate security business, but when the call came from his old friend
Jerry Berry to join the Benson defense team, Laws jumped.

For four years, Berry himself had paid his dues on the
other side of the aisle, prosecuting, among others, a co-
caine-dealing bank president and a triple murderer. Like
D'Alessandro, the schoolboy Berry did not have a burning
desire to be another Clarence Darrow. As a teenager, he
was on his high school wrestling team and worked as a
mail sorter in Miami, a dishwasher at Walgreen's and a
stockboy at K mart. He graduated from Miami Coral Park
High with a 1.6 grade average and worked his way
through junior college as a heavy-equipment operator,
then through law school polling consumers at a shopping
center about jock itch for a marketing research firm. Yet
this time he graduated Phi Beta Kappa.

Sturdy, short, prematurely balding Jerry Berry was eager to play his supporting role as McDonnell's co-counsel
in the Benson drama. The papers wasted no time in pointing out that the thirty-two-year-old attorney bore more
than a passing resemblance to Beaver Cleaver.

On February 12, the defense won a small if inadvertent
victory. Hayes ruled that, if not out of the region, the case
would at least be tried in Fort Myers and not in Naples.
The judge's grudging decision had nothing to do with
McDonnell's fevered motions, or any legal issue, for that
matter. The Benson case was being moved out of Naples'

Collier County Courthouse because building inspectors
had discovered asbestos in the ceiling. The structure
would have to be gutted.

Benson, meantime, had made the most of his impris-
onment. He seemed to adjust quickly to his eight-by-nine-
foot cell, keeping his high-top tennis shoes tucked
squarely under his metal cot and arranging his copies of
the *Wall Street Journal* chronologically in neat piles. His
favorite chess partner was a cocaine smuggler. Behind his
back, the guards called their most celebrated prisoner
"Boom Boom."

✦ ✦ ✦

Electronics genius Guido Dal Molin was not going to walk
away this time. On July 2, 1986, he was charged with
shooting his best friend twice and then, while the victim
begged to be taken to the hospital, driving around for
thirty minutes until he was certain the man had bled to
death. The following afternoon, the victim's pickup truck
was found parked on the shoulder of a remote country
road outside Naples. His body was stretched out in the
back. The clothes he wore were almost completely satu-
rated with blood.

On his long list of witnesses, McDonnell now had a
man who not only had once been picked up for making a
nuclear bomb but now was charged with a particularly
cold-blooded murder. But Dal Molin had no intention of
staying behind bars. He told his jailers that he could escape, and that he would. They believed him. The twenty-
million-dollar jail was less than a year old, and jail chief
Lou Gibbs figured Dal Molin knew the new computer-

controlled security system "better than the guy who installed it. He's way above us in electronics," Gibbs told
his guards. "Eventually, he's going to have the upper
hand."

Chapter 44

From the fifth floor of the stucco-walled Lee County Courthouse, ingeniously angled windows offer a wraparound view of all that Fort Myers has to offer—pleasure craft plying the mouth of the Caloosahatchee River, escorted by schools of friendly dolphins; languidly swaying palms; billowing white clouds drifting westward like hot-air balloons in a limitless blue sky. Looking down, just across the street, there is an ancient banyan tree so immense that its gnarled trunk stretches perhaps fifty feet in diameter, so that its leaves shade an entire park. It is a reminder that, despite the marinas and the condos and the glass-faced professional buildings, this place was once a swamp and could be one again.

This morning, as he walked into his office on the third floor of the courthouse, State Attorney D'Alessandro was taken aback to see his chief prosecutor, Jerry Brock, still shuffling through some last-minute pretrial preparations. Mr. D had chosen the role of *éminence gris*, hovering in the background while his deputies waged war in court, but he could already see that the Brock brothers had made a crucial tactical blunder. D'Alessandro curtly told them they had better get down to the courtroom early to stake out their turf. Seating arrangements could prove to be of vital importance in this subtle contest of nerves. If the defense team sat at the table on the opposite side of the room, jurors could scrutinize the defendant merely by shifting their eyes, without being obvious about it. If he sat just a few feet away, most of the jurors would have to turn their heads to get a good look at him, thereby risking embarrassing eye contact. Traditionally, the table closest to the jury box was reserved for the prosecution.

"Shopper comin' through." Chief prosecutor Delano "Jerry" Brock pushed his borrowed supermarket cart heaped with papers through the crowd of television cameras, reporters and the merely curious jamming the narrow corridor. Little brother Dwight, Brock's assistant on the case, snapped his gum loudly as he trailed behind. As the Brock brothers trotted into Courtroom A to begin the task of jury selection, McDonnell and company were already in place at the favored right-hand table. A cleaning woman had let them in early. Tradition be damned.

Together, the Brocks seemed the perfect foil for the slick McDonnell. Poor farm boys from Florida's panhandle, Delano and Dwight were named for Presidents and became the first in their family to attend college. Dwight Brock, a certified public accountant and an MBA as well as a lawyer, had joined his brother on D'Alessandro's team four years before. When Mr. D paired them up to prosecute the well-connected owners of an ambulance company for embezzling funds from the county and they won the case, the always-in-control Jerry put his feelings into an aw-shucks letter to his boss. Working with his brother, Jerry wrote, had been the most rewarding experience of his professional life. They had also sent one man to jail for life and his partner to death row for a double murder. Perhaps the Brocks took a special interest in that case because the victims were half-brothers.

Unabashed, they played the country lawyer bit to the hilt. Over the four-week course of the Benson trial, the Brocks would interrogate witnesses in a banjo twang, rock back and forth in their chairs during cross-examination as if they were on front-porch rockers and suck loudly on Luden's cough drops when they weren't furiously chewing Trident gum. Both had thinning sandy-blond hair (Jerry had the habit of constantly running his fingers through what remained of his) and wore ill-fitting off-the-rack suits, but there were differences. Jerry was the taller and skinnier of the two (Dwight's gut now spilled out over his monogrammed belt buckle), and though both wore wire-rimmed spectacles, only Dwight used the pink tie he usually wore to clean his. Jerry's expression generally veered from squint to scowl; Dwight hid behind an enigmatic half grin.

Still, D'Alessandro knew they were a tight fit, and that gave them a decided psychological edge. During the course of eliciting testimony, Dwight often dashed up to whisper something into Jerry's ear—the shared confidences of brothers that sometimes made it look as if the defense had been burdened with the task of battling a two-headed adversary.

In contrast to the down-home, suspender-thumping Brocks, the group gathered around the defense table—both male and female—could have posed for a Brooks Brothers ad. Even Steve Benson, now a trim 180 pounds, was out of his orange prison garb and into a freshly pressed gray suit. His dark hair had a strange quarter-sized patch of gray on top. He shifted nervously in his chair, sometimes fiddling with his gold wedding ring. Debbie and the kids were not to be seen, nor did any other member of the family seem to be in Steve's corner. McDonnell knew this would hardly work in his client's favor, but at least Debbie had not yet gone ahead with her rumored plans to pursue divorce proceedings.

Steve, in the meantime, would have to make do with a sort of surrogate courtroom family assembled directly behind him in the front-row seats reserved for the defense—particularly McDonnell's wife, Nina, and her mother, Mafalda Gray, an aristocratic-looking woman who would lean forward to chat with Steven several times a day. Courtroom regulars baffled by this relationship were soon calling Mrs. Gray "Rent-a-Mom."

Not one to be outgunned at this crucial opening phase of the proceedings, McDonnell had called in two attorneys who specialized in jury selection: Wilbur Smith, a tanned and sleek Michael Douglas look-alike who practiced locally and knew the lay of Lee County, and Margaret Covington. A stunningly attractive blonde from Houston, Covington boasted a Ph.D. in psychology and mathematics as well as a law degree and was considered perhaps the nation's leading authority on how best to select a jury. Her biggest assignment to date had been helping celebrated trial lawyer Richard "Racehorse" Haines pick the jury that acquitted oil millionaire T. Cullen Davis of murdering his stepdaughter in 1979.

Covington, who never strayed from lawyerly pinstripe and gray flannel uniforms, had been found guilty on assault charges by a jury after two men she allegedly hired shot the father of her out-of-wedlock offspring after he refused to pay child support. Minutes after the jury rendered its verdict (one of the two assailants testified that he had been hired by Covington to "break her ex-lover's bones and smash his testicles"), the judge in the case caused a furor by setting the conviction aside for lack of evidence. Even as the Benson case was under way, the court of criminal appeal in Texas upheld the controversial decision by the lower court to reverse the jury's ruling and acquit Covington of all charges. Meantime, she sat in a Fort Myers courtroom, closely monitoring the reactions of potential jurors, and every now and then flashed a reassuring cheerleader's smile across the table at Steven.

Courtroom A was an air-conditioned study in neutral tones; what was not paneled in light pine was upholstered in beige fabric—including the walls. Judge Hayes called the proceedings to order at ten-thirty and introduced all the players. Everyone but Steven stood up and took a little bow; Benson smiled meekly and nodded in the direction of the fifty potential jurors. It took Hayes six minutes to read off the nine-count indictment. Hayes had every intention of attending a convention in Reno (he laughingly referred to it as "judges' school"), and that meant the trial was to take no more than three weeks.

McDonnell wasted no time letting the prospective jurors know he still doubted his client could receive a fair trial in Fort Myers. In a voice hushed for dramatic impact, he confided that he was "afraid to death that I will not be able to give him a fair trial because of media saturation in this case. I beg of you," he went on, hands now chopping the air, "I'm very, very scared. I ask you to look into your heart and your soul and see if you were on trial if you were the kind of person you'd want sitting on the jury."

198

Grandstand opening gestures soon gave way to the homey touch. One potential juror said she was a fan of *Murder, She Wrote.* "Are you as good as Angela Lansbury?" McDonnell joked. When another woman told him she was allergic to newsprint, McDonnell quipped, "There are many people allergic to newsprint, and for more than one reason. By the way, anyone here read the article on this case in *People* magazine? No? Good!" To a lady who said what she remembered most about seeing Benson on television was his orange prison jumpsuit, McDonnell asked, "You don't think it's gonna catch on?" Benson laughed.

McDonnell asked potential jurors if they'd ever planned a vacation on the spur of the moment, and if they believed in ESP. Covington's research had indicated that psychic believers are less likely to vote for conviction, and that people who plan their vacations are more likely to support the death penalty.

A retired engineer told Jerry Brock that he was an avid fisherman. "Fishin' is really two sports," Brock drawled, his hands deep in his pockets. "Fishin' 'em and catchin' 'em." Neither Brock nor McDonnell knew quite how to handle John Henry Todd, a karate black belt whose method of reading the newspaper was to throw away the front page and scan the sports pages, want ads and real estate foreclosures. When Judge Hayes told everyone to "stand up and stretch" during a recess, Todd stood and twisted his right leg around the back of his neck.

There were chilling reminders that this was still a grim business. One candidate, asked if he had formed any preconceptions about the case, answered matter-of-factly: "In my mind, I've already fried him." Steve Benson pretended not to hear, his head bent down as he scribbled notes with

199

his blue-and-white Papermate ballpoint. This was not a mere diversion. Over lunch in the defense conference room and in his basement holding cell in the courthouse, Benson told his lawyers just who he liked and didn't like and why. Steve's life was at stake here, McDonnell reasoned. He ought to have some say.

Three days later, ten women and two men took their places in the jury box, along with two female alternates. Their average age was sixty-one. Among the jurors were two nurses, two mystery buffs, two housewives, an engineer, a construction engineer, three retirees—and a one-time explosives expert.

As the all-Caucasian jury—a white-bread blur of plaid blouses, apple-cheeked faces and gray hair—was sworn in, its members seemed oblivious to the chaos of TV and still photographers pressing their cameras up to the window of the soundproof press box directly above their heads. Safely out of earshot, the Levi's-clad young men crammed into this airless glass booth battled claustrophobia with their own running commentary. "Oh, get off it, Jer." "Steve, oh, Stevie boy, that's it, look this way so we can get a good shot of your face." Another antidote for boredom was focusing the cameras on unsuspecting spectators who had the misfortune of being caught as they dozed or scratched themselves.

While the jurors took their oath, the house at 13002 White Violet Drive was being sold to a retired couple who didn't seem to mind that its previous occupants had been blown to bits in the front drive. The price paid for Margaret's 4,606-square-foot temporary home was $300,000—$55,000 less than the asking price.

Chapter 45

Janet Lee Murphy, her face frozen in a Nancy Reagan smile, clutched her daughter Brenda's tanned, bangled arm and made her way past reporters into the packed courtroom. Heads spun to look at Margaret's redheaded little sister and willowy, dark-eyed Brenda. They were there, Janet said, to lend support to Carol Lynn. A Reserved sign was taped to their second-row seats in a section reserved for friends of the prosecution. As her cousin Steven was led into the courtroom by the bailiff, Brenda, a strikingly attractive woman in her mid-20s, dropped her head, tears rolling down her cheeks. "I hate him," she whispered to her mother. "I hate him."

Jerry Brock hooked his fingers in the vest pockets of his three-piece blue suit and stood before the jury. "I see opening statements," he drawled, "as laying out the pieces in a jigsaw puzzle. It's going to be up to me and you to put that puzzle together." Benson stared coldly into space as Brock read off the litany of indictments in his country lawyer's singsong, then spent forty minutes lay-

ing out some of the jigsaw pieces: Steven's alleged financial shenanigans, an hour-long trip to buy coffee and
doughnuts that should have taken fifteen minutes, a telltale palm print. There would be evidence to prove beyond
a reasonable doubt that Steven Benson was guilty of bru-
tally extinguishing the lives of his mother and brother, and
trying to murder his sister.

Then it was McDonnell's turn. He buttoned his jacket
as he walked slowly up to the jury, then tugged at the
French cuffs of his button-down shirt and began. "We
have heard an interesting story this morning. I suggest to
you the evidence will show that Steven Benson was the
loving son of Margaret Benson, the peacemaker in the
family, the man who took over the family when he lost
his father, the only one who did not fight physically tooth
and nail, drawing blood," he said, walking over to the
defense table and placing his hand on his client's shoulder. "He was called upon to settle the disputes between
the rest of the family members. The evidence will show
that Steven Benson is a family man—married with three
delightful children. Mr. Brock found it necessary to read
to you these redundant and cumulative charges. We can
stack charge upon charge upon charge but that isn't evidence." Benson, now shaking with sobs, dabbed his eyes
with a linen handkerchief. It was the first display of any
sort of emotion the jury had seen. Janet's daughter Brenda
shook her head, leaned over and stuck her finger down
her throat à la Joan Rivers.

"I'd like you to look at this man, my friend, the man
who never became angry with his family. The state is saying that Steve Benson, the man who never became angry,
who never, ever fought with his family, on July 9, 1985,
walked out in front of his house in broad daylight and

destroyed —or attempted to destroy—*every single member of his family* for *no good reason.* The state would have you believe Steven wanted to kill these people because his mother wanted to look at the books." McDonnell paused for dramatic effect.

"The evidence," he continued, "will show that there is no evidence. We do not know who committed this crime, and we will not know even after the trial is over. . . . Yes, indeed, Steven was at the wrong place at the wrong time. Steven was at the left front of the car when it exploded, and he tried to drag his mother from the vehicle in the face of multiple explosions." McDonnell began hammering away at the investigation, charging that evidence was ignored, leads not followed. Because of such sloppiness, he went on, "what happened is not clear. But one thing is clear: Steven is an innocent man."

It remained for McDonnell to delicately raise the issue of Scott. "I feel so badly for the Benson family because this is indeed a great tragedy," he said solemnly. "I do not intend to speak ill of the dead, but you will hear of Scott's involvement in the sale and smuggling of illegal drugs. When all is said and done, you'll be able to look at Mr. Brock and say Steven is an innocent man."

The day's parade of prosecution witnesses—all law-enforcement officers—was about to begin. Each trooped in to describe what he saw when he arrived at Quail Creek, pointing out his position on an aerial color blow-up of the house on White Violet Drive taken just a few hours after the blast. The photo, displayed on an easel between the witness stand and the jury box, showed the Suburban and the bodies covered with sheets. Even from the altitude at which the photo was taken, the blackened craters were clearly visible. The day after the murders,

Collier County sheriff's deputy Rene Vila testified, Wayne Kerr arrived with a briefcase to pick up some papers.

Steve crossed and uncrossed his legs beneath the defense table, turning to smile at McDonnell's wife as she brought them coffee in huge Styrofoam cups. She wore a tight beige suit and toted a canvas bag with *Physical* scrawled across it in pink.

Kim Beegle, clad in a lacy white silk pantsuit, might have been Humbert Humbert's fantasy nymphet as she pushed her silken blond hair behind her ears and bounced onto the stand almost cheerfully. Her attitude soon changed.

What was Scott's mood the week before his death, the week he was training for his first U.S. Open?

"He was very happy, skipping around the house and acting like a little kid."

Jerry Brock led her through the shopping trip to Edison Mall, to the restaurants and bars and back home that night before the blasts. All the while, the dog Buck had been with Scott and Kim.

"Have you seen Buck lately?" he asked.

"No. He was like a little kid to us, he traveled around with us. We took him everywhere."

"Did Buck have any obedience training," Brock asked, "any protection training?"

"Yes," Kim replied softly. Judge Hayes asked her to take the microphone off its stand and hold it close enough to her mouth so she could be heard. Janet and Brenda, wearing mother-daughter outfits in black-and-yellow polka dots, smiled benignly from the second row.

"Did he make sounds during the night?" Brock continued.

"Yes, that's what he was trained for. Every time the

security guy drove by at night, Buck barked. He barked at the golfers on the course." Had someone sneaked onto the property to plant the bombs, Kim insisted, Buck would surely have made a racket.

"On the morning of July 9, what awakened you?"

"A loud noise. The windows in the house shook."

"What did you do?"

"I looked out the window and could see this golf guy running. Then I leaned over," she said, choking back the tears, "and I could see the truck engulfed in flames. I knew it was Scott. . . . When I got outside, the first thing I saw was Carol Lynn. She had blood all over. Steven was sitting on the steps and he had his head in his hands. Then I went over to Scott. . . . I stopped and told Steven Scott was dead. He wouldn't even look at me or say anything. . . ."

Brock slipped a color snapshot out of a plain white envelope and handed it to Kim. It had been taken less than an hour after the bombings. "Do you recognize the individual depicted in this photograph?"

"Yes," replied Kim, finally letting go. *"It's Scott!"* A few feet behind Steven, Janet and Brenda dissolved in tears.

McDonnell went on the offensive quickly. Wasn't Scott a cocaine addict? She had only seen him try it "a couple of times." Hadn't Kim told the police in an earlier deposition that Steven was crying when he saw the carnage? "I didn't see any tears coming out of his eyes, and that to me is crying. If it's my statement, I guess I made it." Hadn't Kim said in that same deposition that Steven was sitting there moaning? Could she demonstrate the moan. Kim held the microphone to her mouth and moaned.

McDonnell had not succeeded in tripping up Kim, but

there would be other witnesses. Counsel for the defense then took off for lunch one block away at his regular table near the piano at Fort Myers' chic Veranda restaurant. Meantime, Jerry and Dwight grabbed sandwiches and cherry Cokes at the second-floor courthouse cafeteria.

As she left the courthouse through the back parking lot, Kim was stopped by a reporter and asked if she had any photos of Scotty. She knelt down on the pavement, obligingly searched through her purse and pulled out a small album. There were snapshots of Scotty playing pool with Kim's brother David, of her and Scott with Buck, partying with friends. Still kneeling, she looked up and handed them to the reporter. Tears were streaming down her face.

Chapter 46

There were new faces among the spectators in the packed courtroom—six men and women who had answered an ad in the paper and wound up being handpicked by Margaret Covington to serve on a secret "mirror jury." The mirror jury was selected to reflect as closely as possible the actual jury, and the job of its members was to record their personal reactions to the testimony and report them each evening to McDonnell and Berry. They were paid the same hourly wage they received for their regular jobs. In fact, they appeared to have little in common with the real article. One was a pink-coiffed high school English teacher from the Midwest. A younger woman, with long jet-black hair and heavy mascara, was dubbed Cleopatra by reporters, while another mirror juror was a bald man from Las Vegas with a white mustache and a double-pierced right earlobe.

By now the trial had more than its full complement of colorful regulars; among them a soap opera writer in baggy pants and dark glasses, a redhead with a ruby-studded ankle bracelet and a straw fan, and an eighty-three-year-old retiree who always brought along, tucked under his arm, one of his painted wooden duck decoys.

No one among the spectators would forget Carol Lynn's entrance. There were audible gasps as she stood there almost defiantly facing the audience in an elegant beige silk suit, taking her oath from the female court clerk. It was all too perfect. The pronounced scars on her face and neck could be seen from the last row, yet they seemed almost to enhance her beauty. She might have been Grace Kelly cast in the role of a woman disfigured by a jealous lover.

Carol Lynn took her place in the witness box, not ten feet from her brother. During her three hours of testimony, they were not seen to make eye contact once. She leaned forward into the microphone and spoke in a brittle, deliberate voice. Steven rocked back and forth nervously.

Jerry Brock was determined to squeeze every incriminating detail out of his star witness about that bloody morning. She now unhesitatingly referred to Scott as "my son."

"Scott leaned down toward the front like he was ready to turn the key and immediately following that, I was surrounded by this orange thing. I felt I was being pushed back in the seat."

"Did you know what happened?" Brock asked.

"No, I didn't. I thought I was being electrocuted. . . . There was this thing all around you. I don't know how to explain it. . . . It was just awful. I pushed my eyes open and I saw my son lying on the ground and I knew something was wrong. He had his eyes closed and a little blood on his face. . . . There was blood on his face, and I suddenly thought: He's dead." She recalled looking up and "seeing my brother, Steven, standing on the walk. He was facing the Suburban and staring straight ahead. I couldn't understand why he wasn't coming over to help me." Then, "Steven's eyes opened really wide. He had been standing really still. Suddenly his eyes opened and his mouth dropped and he raced toward the house. . . ."

McDonnell went on the offensive, and so did Carol Lynn. As he had with Kim, the defense lawyer zeroed in on inconsistencies between her early statements and her court testimony. Carol Lynn proved to be his match.

"Mrs. Kendall, is it true that you're not sure at what point Steven gave Scott the keys?"

"No, it's not true."

"Did you not tell Agent Nowicki in July of 1985 that you were not sure when Steven gave Scott the keys?"

"I don't remember the question or the answer. Steven handed Scott the keys through the window of the automobile."

"Didn't you tell Agent Nowicki," McDonnell persisted, "at the time that you only saw Steven out of the corner of your eye?"

"That was almost a year ago. . . . Steven was in my line of sight. . . . I could see him, but I wasn't looking directly *at* him."

"Didn't you tell investigators on the day of the bombing that . . ."

"I was in the hospital under sedation in critical condition at the time." Carol Lynn pursed her lips in anger.

"Mrs. Kendall, isn't it true that you observed Steven attempt to pull your mother from the vicinity of the car?"

Carol Lynn was growing more impatient with McDonnell's line of questioning. "I can't say that. At that point I didn't even know where my mother was. In fact I

was terrified that my mother had been stuck in the burning automobile and burned up. I was asking everybody
that I could where she was and if she had gotten out of
the car. . . ."

McDonnell was now reading from the transcript. "Did
you recall telling Agent Nowicki on July 27 that at one
point 'Steven started to go into the car, I guess after my
mother'?"

"I have no way of knowing if that's what is in the
transcript or if that's what you're trying to make the jury
think is in the transcript."

McDonnell obliged, picking up the huge bound volume and setting it down in front of the witness. He
pointed to the statement in question, and told her to take
her time going over it. "Did you make the statement that
is reflected there?"

Carol Lynn read the page closely, then paused. "Before
I start answering the question," she said, "I have to say
that at the time . . . ."

McDonnell cut her short. "Your Honor, will you in-
struct the witness to answer the question?"

Before McDonnell could finish, Carol Lynn exploded.
"I am answering the question," she insisted angrily. The
decibel level was mounting as she shouted over the defense lawyer. *I am not going to have you distort the answer
by not allowing me to answer the question completely!*"

Ever so gently, Judge Hayes told her to go ahead and
answer the question. "Yes, I did make that statement;
however, at the time the statement was made I had already been informed that my mother's body had been
thrown to the other side of the car. . . . I was making the
assumption with the knowledge he was going around to
that side of the car to my mother."

"At that time Steve was screaming?"

"I could not hear him. There was noise. . . . It sounded as though he was making lamenting types of sounds. His body was extremely agitated."

McDonnell repeated the question. "Was he screaming?"

"Yeah, I guess you could put it that way."

Wasn't it true, McDonnell wanted to know, that when Steven started back to the house to get the tape measure, he was standing only a few feet in front of the car when the bombs went off? Carol Lynn paused, then replied almost wistfully, "I can see them right now. I can see Mother and Scott sitting there—and I can see the empty walkway." When it was all over, Carol Lynn had won. She had not been shaken one iota in her testimony. Then, after she somehow managed to escape the press, she ducked into the ladies' room and she cried.

Chapter 47

It seemed more than just faintly ironic that the two most important witnesses against Steve Benson would both be named Kendall. Looking professorial, the ATF's Frank Kendall stood at an easel set up facing the jury, and used a yardstick to point out each of the sixty similar traits between the palm prints found on the pipe invoices and Benson's palm prints. Numbered arrows had been drawn between each common loop and swirl so that even from their vantage point the jurors could follow Kendall's explanation. What did this mean? "The prints," answered Kendall unequivocally, "were made by one and the same person."

There was nothing McDonnell could do to shake Kendall's testimony, but when he emerged from the courtroom to speak to waiting television reporters, the defense attorney insisted that he would prove his client was nowhere near Hughes Supply at the time the pipes were supposed to have been purchased. "There's no question in our mind," said McDonnell, whose chiseled features and whiter-than-white grin suited the cameras beautifully, "Steven Benson did not buy the pipes." So who put his prints on the receipts? "I don't know," he said, shrugging. "I don't have any answers. I only have doubts." He devoutly hoped the jury was developing some of its own.

The emotional strain was already beginning to register on the weary faces of the jurors when Jerry Brock handed them the photographs. If they had hoped to shock the ten women and two men with the graphic evidence that Margaret and Scott had been horribly mutilated by the blast, the Brock brothers succeeded. As the photos were passed from one juror to the next, each visibly struggled to maintain his or her composure. One woman put her hand to her mouth when she looked at the photo of Margaret laid out on a medical examiner's slab, her face virtually torn away. Another gathered all the photographs in her lap as she looked straight ahead, then, steeling herself, she looked down and shuffled through them quickly.

McDonnell objected that the grisly photos had nothing to do with Steve Benson's guilt or innocence. "They're gruesome," he said, "they're not necessary. There's no reason why people should be subjected to that sort of thing."

Judge Hayes disagreed. And Jerry Brock insisted, "I think they were necessary for the jury to fully comprehend the severity of the crime that was committed here. The jury has the right to see the whole picture."

So did the public at large, or at least so thought the managers of both local television stations in Fort Myers. WINK and WEVU began preempting regular daytime shows to air the trial live. Soon their switchboards were flooded with hundreds of calls, some from viewers thanking the stations for bumping Merv Griffin, but most complaining that the real-life courtroom saga of money, family and murder was causing them to miss their favorite soaps. Among those glued to their TV was Carol Lynn, holed up under her aunt Janet Murphy's name in a suite at the elegant, pink-and-white Naples Beach Club. To those who called asking for Janet, Carol Lynn—now the most sought-after interviewee in town—identified herself as the house-keeper.

Chapter 48

Al Gleason's account of how he scoured the Benson driveway for bomb fragments and then painstakingly constructed a facsimile of the device was clearly boring the jury; one juror nodded off, another repeatedly stifled her yawns. But no one yawned when Gleason, with the help of Jerry Brock, entered the replica into evidence. There were gasps when Brock picked up the foot-long, four-inch-diameter pipe bomb and, grasping it with both hands, strained to lift it onto the witness table. Brock then slowly carried the sinister-looking chunk of galvanized steel over to the jury so that they could get an idea of the size and weight of the murder weapon. Filled with gunpowder, such a pipe bomb would weigh twenty-seven pounds.

◆ ◆ ◆

Dwight Brock rocked back and forth on his heels, his hands jammed firmly in his pockets. Wayne Kerr was explaining to the jury why Margaret had called him down to Naples to go over Meridian's finances. Kerr had lost his battle to avoid testifying by invoking lawyer-client privilege. Judge Hayes had ruled that Kerr's conversations with the deceased Margaret Benson were no longer confidential in view of the seriousness of the crime, and ordered Kerr to answer the prosecution's subpoena. Kerr wore a two-tone shirt and his hair was unfashionably long. He breathed through his mouth into the open microphone—that unnerving deep-sea-diver sound. He would not, however, be asked to testify about his conversations with the defendant. Those discussions, the court agreed, were covered by attorney-client privilege.

Unquestionably, Kerr's testimony was key to establishing Steven's motive for the murders. He was not only the one person who had extensive knowledge concerning the Benson family finances, but he also knew Margaret's state of mind in the months leading up to July 9. And, even as he took the stand against Steven, he would insist that he was still a friend of the accused.

Under questioning by Dwight Brock, Kerr was interrupted again and again as McDonnell jumped in with objections, taking the issue to the bench. Kerr bided his time sipping water and wiping sweat from his brow with a handkerchief. For the first time since jury selection, Steven was taking notes, leafing anxiously through a black-bound volume of transcripts roughly the size of the Manhattan telephone directory, trying to catch Kerr in some deviation from his previous depositions.

"How did Margaret react when she saw Steven's new house?" asked Brock.

"She was surprised."

"Surprised?"

216

"She was surprised at the size of the house. She was surprised at the tennis court. She was surprised at the swimming pool. She was surprised that his blue Datsun was sitting in the driveway."

"Did she inquire of you what her options were relative to this house?"

"Yes. She asked if she could secure any of the previous loans that she had made to Steven through this house."

"Did you converse with Mrs. Benson on the return during the trip all the way back to Naples?"

"Yes I did."

"What was her attitude during this trip?"

"She was angry."

"What do you mean by angry?"

"Well, she was angry that she had seen this house and she was angry about Meridian Marketing . . ."

McDonnell was objecting repeatedly, calling for bench conferences out of earshot of the jury and the spectators. He fought hard to keep the jury from hearing Kerr's testimony regarding Margaret's feelings of anger toward her son.

Dwight persisted, leading the jury through the events leading up to the explosion that rocked the house on White Violet Drive the morning of July 9.

"How loud was the blast that you heard?"

"It was a loud blast. . ."

"Do you remember anything else about it," asked Dwight.

"Yes. Marty Taylor, Margaret's secretary, was right across from me . . . diagonally across from me and I said 'Oh, my god, what was that?' And she sort of looked at me in a state of disbelief. . . I thought possibly one of the Lotuses had exploded . . . I walked to a corner of the Florida room that adjoined the kitchen . . . I thought I heard something pelting against those windows."

"When you got to the front door what did you see?" Brock went on, asking the witness to refer to the enlarged photograph of the house on White Violet Drive.

"I really didn't get to the front door. I basically walked into the living room foyer area and saw Steven coming in the door . . . and he said 'Call an ambulance.' He seemed to be out of control—his hands were shaking very violently—and in a state of great concern. I think I asked Marty Taylor what was the emergency number . . . and I proceeded to call that number and state there had been an accident at 13002 White Violet Drive."

"Where was Steve during this telephone conversation?"

"He was right there with me."

"He didn't go back outside?" Brock asked in mock amazement.

"No."

"How long did Steve stay with you?"

"He stayed with me the entire time. Sometime during that conversation there was another bomb that went off that shook the house."

"This was while Steve was still in the house that the second bomb went off?"

"Yes."

"Did you ever see Mr. Benson with a paramedic?"

"Yes I did . . . a gentleman came over and administered a blood pressure test."

"Did you see any injuries on Steven that day?"

"No."

"Did you see any blood on him that day?"

"No."

This little detour of Brock's in fact raised serious questions concerning the likelihood that Steven could have escaped injury altogether if he hadn't known about the bombs beforehand. McDonnell's cross-examination was brief, and, from the standpoint of his client, fruitless.

Leading the financial attack, Dwight, the CPA Brock brother, called ATF auditor Diana Galloway to the stand. McDonnell kicked one booted foot up on the table and, twisting his wedding band, leaned back to listen. Steven took a roll of mints out of his pocket, carefully unwrapped one, placed it in his mouth and, without moving his mouth, continued staring straight ahead. Galloway produced charts, diagrams and stapled pamphlets for the jurors so they could follow as she traced the flow of funds from Margaret's accounts through Meridian into Steven's pocket. The final tabulation, by Galloway's best determination, was $85,692.43.

"Do you have any information that Steven isn't entitled to the money?" asked McDonnell.

"No."

"You're not saying that Steven stole this money?"

"I can't make that statement."

"Are you telling us that Steven Benson blew up his mother, his brother and his sister for $85,000?" McDonnell demanded.

"I can't make that determination," Galloway answered coolly.

◆ ◆ ◆

McDonnell had more success after Stephen Dancsec testified about the wake for Margaret and Scott in Naples and

Benson's curious admission to the mourners that he used to blow up pipe bombs as a kid in Lancaster.

"Didn't you tell me that unless you were paid," sneered McDonnell, "you were going to hold a press conference and really hurt Steven?"

Benson's curly-haired former employee squirmed in his seat, then conceded he had—but only because he and the other Meridian employees were urged to keep the company going after Margaret's death and were never paid for sixty days' work. "I just felt we were being dealt a raw deal."

"Do you hold any animosity toward the defendant today?" Jerry Brock asked Dancsec in redirect.

"No, sir."

McDonnell, as he had every day in the two weeks since the trial began, emerged from the main courtroom entrance to work the press, while the Brocks quietly wheeled their shopping cart filled with evidence through a side door. Today, McDonnell's Madison Avenue grin was even more blinding than usual. The Brocks, he proclaimed triumphantly, had "shot themselves in the foot." Off-camera, he likened the prosecution case to the "old joke about the guy who walks into a store and tries on a suit that doesn't fit.

" 'The sleeves are too long,' says the customer.

" 'Well,' the tailor replies, 'just sort of scrunch down and hold your arms like this.'

" 'Okay, but the pants are too short.'

" 'No, just hunch over and turn your body like that. See? Perfect!'

"Later, two men see this guy walking down the street in his new suit, all bent and hunched over. One of them says, 'Look at that poor, deformed man.'

" 'Yeah,' says the other guy, 'but what a great-fitting suit!' That's what this case is, gentlemen—a suit that doesn't fit."

How was his client holding up under the pressure? reporters wanted to know. "He's devastated," said McDonnell solemnly. "My heart goes out to this man."

◆ ◆ ◆

There was still one loose thread remaining in the Brock brothers' case—to convince the jury that the gangly, bony-shouldered Benson that sat here today could be the same portly man, shown in the composite drawing, who bought the pipes at Hughes Supply. Enter Lieutenant Jackie Gant, a big-bellied good ole boy in a sky-blue western suit and jet-black Roy Orbison sideburns.

"Do you know Steven Benson?" Jerry Brock asked.

"I held hands with him for thirty minutes." Gant went on to explain that he fingerprinted and photographed Benson when he was arrested. "He was much heavier then. I'm a couple of inches shorter than Steven Benson, and he was bigger—heavier—than me. No, his face is thinner. He's definitely trimmed down."

The prosecution rested its case, and the jury was excused so that McDonnell could make the pro forma motion that Hayes set Benson free. "We ask you, Your Honor, to make a difficult and courageous decision and enter a judgment of acquittal for Steven Benson."

Almost before McDonnell had finished, Hayes turned him down. "There is sufficient evidence for the jury to conclude there is guilt. A motion for acquittal cannot be granted." Once he'd brought down the gavel, Hayes barely took the time to shed his robes as he flew out the back door of his chambers. Tossing his jacket over his shoulder, he headed straight for his parking space, where his aristocratically beautiful wife was waiting for him. They threw their arms around one another, climbed into their silver-gray Jeep and headed off into the flamingo-pink sunset.

Chapter 49

It was a little after 2:20 A.M.—five minutes after the last bed check—when Guido Dal Molin jammed the lock of his cell and sprinted to the booking area. Four guards raced after him as Dal Molin ducked into the unlocked control room and punched a sequence of buttons on the electronic console. The door behind him slammed shut on the guards, and the door, the garage door and the gate leading to the outside swung open. His jailers trapped behind their own gates, Dal Molin laughed as he raced to freedom. All the police saw were his heels.

This was the very week Dal Molin was to have told the Benson jury what he knew about Scott. The disappearance of a witness like Dal Molin at this moment in the trial seemed almost too coincidental. Speculation ran rampant that Dal Molin may have had an accomplice. But McDonnell was careful not to exaggerate the importance of his missing witness, and with good reason. He had no assurance that, once on the stand, Dal Molin had any intention of talking. So long as he was on the loose, attracting media attention to the seamy world of the dead Scotty's friends, Dal Molin remained an unexpected blessing for the defense.

Chapter 50

Steven got up in his holding cell in the basement of the Lee County Courthouse around six-thirty A.M. this Saturday, July 26, and, as he had for the past three weeks, put on one of the two suits that were pressed after each wearing. This was the day the defense was to start calling its witnesses. It was also Steven's thirty-fifth birthday. There would be no one to see him; inmates in his cellblock were allowed visitors only on Sunday mornings, and then only for two hours. No exceptions.

Actually, there was no one to make an exception for. Debbie, as she had so many times before, fled home to Wisconsin weeks before the trial started. There she gathered hay and milked cows on her brother's dairy farm in Westby, and guarded Natalie and the twins from the prying press. Debbie wanted desperately to forget what was happening to her husband thirteen hundred miles away. Yet she continued to withdraw her monthly allotment from the children's trust fund.

Well, their daddy was used to fending for himself. In

truth, he had always been alone. Stationed in her customary front-row aisle seat, "Rent-a-Mom" Mafalda Gray
leaned over the dock, smiled warmly at Steven and
mouthed the words "Happy birthday."

Brenda Turnbull bounced onto the stand in a tight
white knit dress and flashed a broad grin at her former
boss. She testified that Steve Benson could not have
bought the pipes from Hughes Supply to blow up Margaret and Scott because he was with her in the Meridian
trailer at the time. McDonnell stood at an easel and used
a green Magic Marker to write down the dates and times.
Turnbull also denied there was any talk of Steve making
bombs during the wake at the Pittman Funeral Home.
Dwight Brock made a little paper airplane out of a gum
wrapper while his brother cupped his ear like an old-time
radio announcer to hear Turnbull's testimony. The two
brothers swiveled in unison.

On July 5, 1985, said Turnbull, Benson did not leave
the office until four-fifty—at least an hour and twenty minutes after he allegedly walked into Hughes Supply wearing a baseball hat and bought the two end caps he used
to make the bombs. He couldn't have bought the pipes
themselves at four-thirty on July 8 because she saw him
walk past her on the way out of the office fifty minutes
after that—around five-twenty. She was certain about the
times, she said, "because I'm a clock-watcher."

Jerry Brock sauntered up to Turnbull, shaking his
head, his hands in his pockets.

"So you're a clock-watcher."

"Yes."

"Tell me, when you get home at night, don't you have
a crick in your neck from looking down at your watch so
much?"

In her deposition, Brock pointed out, Turnbull told de-

fense lawyers that Benson had left the office between 3:30
P.M. and 4:00 P.M. on July 5. There was no way she could
be certain Benson hadn't sneaked out to buy the pipes,
was there? "You didn't sit there guarding the door to see
that he would go out for ten or fifteen minutes, did you?"
asked Jerry Brock.

"No."

"You cannot tell us with absolute certainty that he did
not leave, can you?"

"No."

"In fact, you have no earthly idea when the defendant
left the office, do you? Yes? Then tell me, *specifically*, where
was the big hand pointin' and where was the little hand
pointin'? You have no earthly idea when Steven Benson
left the office, do you?"

Steven, sitting ramrod straight, leaned over and calmly
poured himself a glass of water from an insulated pitcher.

After all, Brock went on, there was no reason for Turnbull to pay such close attention to Benson's comings and
goings. "You didn't know Scott and Mrs. Benson were
going to be blown out of this world the next day, did
you?"

Brock had not finished chipping away at Turnbull's
credibility. "Were you the only Meridian employee paid
after the bombing?" Brock wanted to know.

"No, Wayne Kerr came in July 15 and paid everyone."

"But you were the only one paid after that, however?"

"They had husbands and wives," Turnbull replied, a
new edge of defiance to her voice. "I had to pay the rent."

"You're not implying that they didn't have to pay the
bills, are you?"

"No, but they had husbands and wives working as
well."

Brock then shifted to the wake, and whether investigators had ever asked her about Steven making bombs. She said she did not remember.

"It wasn't an easy thing," said Turnbull, now sobbing into a Kleenex. One of the jurors looked at her disdainfully and shook her head.

"We tend to forget things, don't we?"

"Yes," she said softly.

Steven crossed his legs and tucked his left hand between his thighs. His expression seemed oddly imperious.

◆ ◆ ◆

With Turnbull's testimony shattered, McDonnell now turned his sights on the dead Scotty. But when the defense attorney told the court that he intended to call several surprise witnesses—witnesses that the prosecution would first have to take depositions from—Judge Hayes exploded. "This is bush league law," he seethed. "Damn bush league, and I don't like it." The muscles in Hayes' jaw rippled as he struggled to regain control. "In the middle of a trial, to tender a witness for deposition is . . . unfortunate." To everyone's astonishment, Jerry Berry, McDonnell's co-counsel, loudly defended the move, but the judge cut him short. "There is no point in making the system look any worse than it already does."

McDonnell waited until he was bearded by the press to return the fire. "He seems very much concerned with attending an upcoming judicial conference," said counsel for the defense. "I think it is very important to him and his personal career. I would hate to get in the way of his advancement." Now resigned to missing at least part of his "judges' school" in Reno, Hayes insisted that "school or no school, the trial comes first." McDonnell had put the judge on the spot, and Hayes was unlikely to forget it.

Chapter 51

He lay perfectly motionless in the underbrush along the roadway, listening to the sound of his own heartbeat and the barking of police dogs. Guido Dal Molin held his breath as the barking grew louder, so loud that his break for freedom seemed about to end. They were sniffing within three feet of him—but, amazingly, they passed on by.

Once the barking had begun to fade in the distance, Dal Molin scrambled through the underbrush, making his way along the East Tamiami Trail to a local shopping center. Climbing up the drainpipe to the roof of a K mart, he hunkered down beneath the air-conditioning unit, out of sight of the police helicopters that hovered overhead.

◆ ◆ ◆

Tom Fife was on his way home when he spotted Dal Molin standing in the parking lot of a small bar called The Ship's Inn. Fife, a Naples plainclothesman, called "Barney" after the bumbling deputy played by Don Knotts on television's *Andy Griffith Show*, got out of his car, walked up to Dal Molin and told him he was under arrest. It would not be that easy. Dal Molin began grappling for Fife's gun, biting Fife's hands again and again until his right thumb was nearly torn off. A rangy young passerby rushed to Fife's aid, pulling a knife from under his shirt and brandishing it at the crazed young genius. Together, they wrestled Dal Molin to the ground. He had managed to elude capture for nearly four days.

Back at the Collier County jail, Barney Fife's hands were stitched up and his blood screened for tetanus and AIDS. To celebrate his heroic capture of Naples' number one fugitive, jail guards wheeled out a cake. The inscription constituted one final, inadvertently hysterical indignity: *To Bonnie, for a job well done.*

◆ ◆ ◆

For McDonnell, it was a time of reckoning. Dal Molin, as he had feared, wasn't talking—on the stand or off. His role in the Benson drama was speculative at best, and given His Honor's rather unsympathetic reaction to other eleventh-hour witnesses, calling Dal Molin as a witness for the defense now might backfire. The man who once built an atomic bomb and was now charged with murdering his friend had been the subject of the most publicized wild-goose chase in Florida history. The defense would have to rely on other witnesses to paint a grim picture of Scott. Steven's life depended on it.

Chapter 52

It would not be difficult to prove that Scott was a behavior problem—Carol Lynn had said as much about her newly acknowledged son in her depositions—or that he had been a chronic abuser of drugs. But McDonnell knew all too well he was treading a fine line between defending his client and defaming the defenseless dead. It was a chance he would have to take.

Harry Hitchcock sat out the trial with Carol Lynn at the Naples Beach Club, watching the testimony on television. Outside, the sound of children playing on the beach could be heard above the roar of the gulf.

Ed Malone the roofer, Scott's former tennis partner, testified that a man "from out of town" had said that Scott owed him thirty thousand dollars for a kilo of cocaine.

"He was talking about what would happen to people if they didn't pay. That's when Scott Benson's name came up."

And what would happen to Scott?

"He said if Scott didn't pay like the rest of them, he could lose his fanny."

Other witnesses were hauled out of jail to talk about little more than Scott's pot smoking and fondness for laughing gas. "And he was out there," Dwight Brock said incredulously, "just totin' around this big ol' scuba tank in the parkin' lot and just in front of God and everybody he was suckin' down this here nitrous oxide?" Even Steven laughed.

"When you used this here laughing gas," Dwight went on, "did it make you want to go home and blow up your mama?"

◆ ◆ ◆

Speaking in the clipped accent of her native Boston, Margaret's former secretary Joyce Quinn softly recalled that morning in September of 1983 when Scott went berserk at the Port Royal house and attacked Margaret—the incident that ended with Scott's being carted off to the psychiatric ward. Then defense counsel Berry took the microcassette out of the envelope Quinn had placed it in that afternoon and played it for the stunned courtroom:

"Mother, I don't have to do anything. I give you all the respect you deserve."

"What do you mean by that, Scott? *Scott?*"

"Say it over—'The dog is Scott Benson's. The dog is Scott Benson's. Say it right into the tape. . . . Can you understand that? Huh? Do you? *Do you?*"

"Get your hands off—" There were sounds of a struggle, then silence.

The ghostly voices hung in the room for several mo- ments after Berry shut off the recorder. Shaken, several of the jurors wept. Whether from grief or remorse, so did Steven Benson.

Chapter 53

Seconds before closing arguments were to begin, Harry Hitchcock walked slowly to the front of the courtroom on Janet's arm. He paused to lean on the railing before settling into a front-row aisle seat. His shock of white hair caught Steven's eye, and for a lingering moment Benson seemed to seek a glimmer of acknowledgment from his grandfather. It never came. Boppa sat with his lips parted slightly, his eyes revealing nothing. His hands would leave his sides only once during Jerry Brock's summation, to adjust his tie clip. The clip, which Hitchcock always wore, was fashioned in the shape of a fish, a symbol of his Christian faith.

"The events leading up to this horrible crime," Brock began, gripping the lectern as he faced the jury, "began unfolding back in January 1985." As Benson nervously wrung his hands, Brock laboriously retraced every step leading up to the murders. Nearly an hour later, Brock ventured his own explanation as to why the beige van was parked so close to the doomed Suburban: "Why? Because the *records* were in the van. Steven expected the Suburban to blow up the van as well. Remember, the van was parked so close that the side was splattered with blood and flesh."

Then Brock recalled Benson's first words to Steve Hawkins when Hawkins arrived with Debbie that bloody Tuesday morning. "He asks Hawkins, 'How much money did we make today?' I submit," Brock said, holding up the fingers of both hands, "almost ten million dollars."

Brock waved a photo in front of the jury. It clearly showed, amid the charred bits of wreckage strewn about the bombing site, a tape measure—the tape measure Steve Benson said he was going back into the house to retrieve. Still, McDonnell had insisted police had never found the real murderer—someone who wanted to even a score with Scott. "Mr. McDonnell's problem is that he was looking everywhere else," Brock roared, slamming his fist on the defense table inches from Benson, "except right here in front of him."

McDonnell shot to his feet and stood ramrod straight, his teeth clenched in an angry scowl. Tempers cooled. The lawyer for the defense straightened his plum-colored tie and placed a stack of black folders atop the lectern. Then he turned to a blackboard set up in front of the jury and, saying nothing, scrawled a single word in red letters. The word was *Suspicion*.

"You are being sold a suit that does not fit," McDonnell told the jury. "The prosecution is trying to fit a square peg into a round hole, to make a silk purse of a sow's ear." Carol Lynn was "a woman who does not deserve to go through what she has gone through, but it is because she went through this traumatic experience her testimony is unreliable." As he debunked each prosecution witness,

each piece of evidence, McDonnell took one of the folders
and with a flourish tossed it onto the defense table.

In Scotty, McDonnell argued, "we have one poor, unfortunate young man running amok, dragging his mother
across the floor, beating his sister and biological mother
on the face *with his fists*. Beyond that, I'll tread no more
on Scotty's memory." Steven was wiping tears from his
eyes. Harry sat motionless, sphinxlike.

"Remember," McDonnell solemnly told the jury,
"you're not angels of vengeance, you're angels of justice.
I'm going to give him to you now," he said, placing his
hand on Benson's shoulder. "Take good care of him." As
he sat down, Benson leaned over and whispered in his
lawyer's ear. "You did a good job," he said.

Chapter 54

At 1:14 P.M. on August 7, 1986, foreman Ernest Henning knocked once on the jury room door. After eleven hours of deliberation, the ten women and two men had reached a verdict. Reporters, crammed into a small room where the famous *Rambo III* tape was being screened, scrambled to their feet and bounded to the courtroom.

There had already been one false alarm, which afforded its moment of drama. Late the night before, bleary-eyed members of the press who had been camping out in the hallways were alerted that the jury was going back into the courtroom. Carol Lynn, in the courtroom for the first time since her testimony, had come expecting to hear firsthand her brother's fate. Steve turned and, with a smirk, locked eyes with Carol Lynn for what seemed like an eternity.

There was no verdict then, however; the jury had merely wanted to have some crucial testimony read back to them. After the jury retired for the night, Carol Lynn walked out, saying nothing to reporters; as photographers pursued her, she turned away from them, holding up her hand to conceal her scarred face.

Today it was the real thing. "This has to be it," said McDonnell. Someone else was sitting at his customary table at the Veranda; he had been too nervous to eat lunch. As one of the bailiffs led Benson in, McDonnell walked up to him and shook his hand. "We've got a verdict," he told Steve. He searched the first few rows in vain for Carol Lynn.

Steven Benson's sister was at the Naples Beach Club with their aunt and their grandfather, watching the drama draw to a close on live television. They were worried that McDonnell had succeeded at creating a smoke screen by shifting the focus to Scotty and his drugs. Suddenly, Harry thought, it was as if Scotty, not Steven, were on trial.

As the jury—basically a collection of bleary-eyed women with pastel sweaters pinned around their necks— filed in, averting their eyes from Benson, McDonnell knew from their faces what their decision would be.

"Have you reached a verdict?"

"We have, Your Honor," foreman Henning replied, handing the bailiff the forms on which the verdicts on each of the nine counts were checked off. Benson tried in vain to make eye contact with the jurors; some bowed their heads. Hayes leafed quickly through the forms before handing them to the court clerk. Her voice quavered as she read off the charges and the verdicts one by one: "On the charge of first-degree, premeditated murder of Margaret Benson, the jury finds the defendant—guilty. On the charge of first-degree murder of Scott Benson—guilty." Guilty . . . guilty . . . guilty . . . guilty . . .

McDonnell clasped his hand on Benson's left shoulder.

"Steven," defense lawyer Berry said reassuringly, "this is only the first battle." Benson nodded. One of the white-haired women who had been attending the trial religiously went up to Benson and reached out her hand. "Steven, I'm so sorry," she whimpered, tears bouncing off the front of her blouse. "I know you're innocent." Steven thanked her and squeezed her hand. "No contact," yelled the bailiff, leading Benson away. *"No contact."*

Jerry Brock made an impassioned plea for the death penalty: "Think in your mind what crime to man is more reprehensible than taking the life of the person who gave him life. It just sends goose bumps down my back." Brock then drew an unfortunate biblical parallel. Judas' betrayal of Christ, he proclaimed, "was nothing to compare to what this defendant did. They weren't even related!"

McDonnell, who now appeared to be almost chastened by defeat, wearily confessed that the murders were heinous. "As Mr. Brock spoke about Jesus, I remembered His words: Forgive them."

The jury split down the middle on whether to pull the switch, leaving it for Hayes to decide Steven Benson's fate: two life sentences for murder, to run consecutively, plus thirty-seven years for attempted murder and arson. Benson would be eligible for parole in forty-nine years.

McDonnell was jubilant. Outside the courtroom, he called the life sentence "a great victory. I've never had a client go to the electric chair and I don't intend to. I don't want to participate in the taking of human life any longer," he added, in an oblique reference to his Vietnam days. What now? a reporter asked. "Now"—McDonnell grinned—"I'm gonna get my children and take them to the beach."

Hayes rushed to board a flight for Reno. He'd just be able to catch the last two weeks of Judges' School.

Epilogue

In the coming months, Carol Lynn would sue to cut Steven Benson's children out of the will and block Tracy Mullins' ongoing paternity suit against Scott's estate. McDonnell would file a series of appeals, holding that the conviction was based on circumstantial evidence.

Judge Hayes, meantime, flatly denied a motion that Benson be allowed to serve out his sentences concurrently—making him eligible for parole in twenty-four years instead of forty-nine. "I feel very comfortable with Mr. Benson sitting there serving two consecutive life terms," said Hayes. "I'd feel very uncomfortable with him serving only one term."

Debbie continued to build a new life for herself and her children in Wisconsin, while back home in Lancaster, Harry would spend the rest of his life wondering if, even as he was presiding at prayer breakfasts, he had somehow neglected the souls of his own family.

◆ ◆ ◆

Today, a single misshapen pine casts a crooked shadow over the family tomb. Inside, soft light gently illuminates the stained-glass window—a depiction of Jesus praying on the Mount of Olives. The inscription reads: NOT MY WILL, BUT THINE BE DONE. Harry had chosen this line of scripture, and it comforted him.

A newer inscription has appeared on the tomb's granite exterior, three haunting characters spray-painted in black:

$ A D

Index